9-14-14

Love and Blessing
Cheryl

x x x x x x x x x x x x x x x x x x x x x x x x x x x x

Knitting, Praying, Forgiving
A Pattern of Love and Forgiveness

x x x x x x x x x x x x x x x x x x x x x x x x x x x

Cheryl Wunsch MEd RNCS

InspiringVoices

Inspiring Voices books may be ordered through booksellers or by contacting:

Inspiring Voices
1663 Liberty Drive
Bloomington, IN 47403
www.inspiringvoices.com
1 (866) 697-5313

ISBN: 978-1-4624-1015-6 (sc)
ISBN: 978-1-4624-1016-3 (e)

Library of Congress Control Number: 2014912176

Printed in the United States of America.

Inspiring Voices rev. date: 7/15/2014

For my mother,
Dorothy Jean Griffin
1924–1971

CONTENTS

Foreword xxxxxxxxxxxxxxxxxxxxxxxxxxxxxxxxxxxxxxxxxxx ix
Acknowledgments xxxxxxxxxxxxxxxxxxxxxxxxxxxxxxxxxxxx xi
Introduction xxxxxxxxxxxxxxxxxxxxxxxxxxxxxxxxxxxxxxxx xiii

Part One
A Forgiveness Journey

Chapter 1   Visits with Anna xxxxxxxxxxxxxxxxxxxxxxxxxx 1
Chapter 2   Forgiveness: A Path to Love xxxxxxxxxxxxxxxxxx 9
Chapter 3   Forgiveness Prayer Shawl xxxxxxxxxxxxxxxxxx 17
Chapter 4   Prayers from the Heart xxxxxxxxxxxxxxxxxxxxx 27

Part Two
A Pattern of Love and Forgiveness

Chapter 5   Remembering: The Person or Group You Want to
             Forgive xxxxxxxxxxxxxxxxxxxxxxxxxxxxxxxxxxx 33
Chapter 6   Gathering: Your Thoughts, Feelings, and Memories xx 39
Chapter 7   Holding: God and Your Journal xxxxxxxxxxxxxxx 45
Chapter 8   Gleaning: Knitting into God's Word-Lectio Divina xx 51
Chapter 9   Transformation xxxxxxxxxxxxxxxxxxxxxxxxxxx 57

Endnotes xxxxxxxxxxxxxxxxxxxxxxxxxxxxxxxxxxxxxxxxxx 65

Appendix A   Scriptures for Knitting into God's Word:
             Forgiveness, Love, Compassion xxxxxxxxxxxxxxx 69
Appendix B   Embracing God's Word, Lectio Divina xxxxxxxxxx 77
Appendix C   Prayer Shawl Card xxxxxxxxxxxxxxxxxxxxxxxx 89
Appendix D   Dorothy's Peace and Forgiveness Prayer Card xxxxxx 93

Through her own personal story of tragedy, heartbreak, and grief, Cheryl Wunsch has written a poignant and unfolding story, sharing with readers her spiritual evolution of forgiveness and personal faith journey. Using the ancient prayer technique of *lectio divina*, readers are guided through spiritual exercises—the framework for the contemplative practice of prayer, meditation, and personal journal keeping.

Weaving in biblical and modern-day quotes, readers are guided through her five core forgiveness foundations of remembering, gathering, holding, gleaning, and transformation. Insights and instructions are given for applying these techniques to create a "love and forgiveness shawl," or some other form of a tangible gift, to honor a person or group.

Threefold blessings to Cheryl! She offers deep-filled insights, inspirations, and contemplative tools for her readers. As a prayer shawl maker myself, [I recognize that] she has laid a new path for creating forgiveness shawls that not only bless the recipient but the prayer shawl maker as well. For anyone who takes up her book, a journal, and set of knitting needles, her message continues to widen the circle of God's universal gifts of forgiveness and unconditional love.

Victoria A. Cole-Galo
Cofounder of the Prayer Shawl Ministry

I want to thank God for the gift of faith and for my three beautiful daughters, two amazing sons-in-law, and two adorable, precious grandsons. I am blessed! A special thank-you to my cousin Meryl, for always encouraging me about my writing, and a loving thank-you to each of my cousins, my two sisters, my brothers-in-law, and my three fantastic nephews and beautiful niece. Thank you for your love.

My deepest gratitude to Daniel Stern, for daring to believe in me. A thank-you to Barbara for your kindness and patience in typing my early handwritten journal notes. When I first met Anna, I wanted to get my amazing miracle experience on paper, and my dear friend and then-colleague Jill typed as I spoke. Thank you, Jill; you always know my heart! I am forever grateful to Sister Jeanne for guiding Dorothy's Peace and Forgiveness Prayer Shawl Ministry after I moved to California. I never could have written this book without your love, support, and feedback. Thank you! Much gratitude to my dear friends Cheryl, Aye, Mary, and Susan, who listened, prayed, and supported my writing for many years. Thank you, Cheryl, for being a beacon of God's light when I would get lost in my writing. Thank you, Marge, for all of the good times while knitting and crocheting shawls and for teaching me how to crochet. I think of you with every ripple shawl I crochet. A special thank-you to our Pennsylvania prayer shawl group. I think of you all with love and prayers.

After moving to California a few years ago, I was blessed and welcomed at my new church, the Church of the Good Shepherd. Thank you to Monsignor Thomas Welbers, my pastor. Thank you, Sister Virginia, for inviting me to organize our church prayer shawl ministry and for your support. My sincere gratitude to all of our prayer shawl knitters and crocheters. A special thank-you to Nicole for your support and prayers—you inspire me—and to Ethel, for always having words of praise for our prayer shawl ministry. My heartfelt thanks to Father Colm O'Ryan, Mary Ann, and each person in our meditation group. Thank you, Annette, for your encouragement and prayers, and my deep gratitude to Sister Audrey for your kindness in correcting my grammar. A thank-you to Jayne and Stephanie, my neighbors and friends, for your encouraging words. A warm thank-you to Father Robert, for your oblate guidance, and to Brother Bede, for deepening my experience in lectio. My sincere thanks to Paula for helping me early on to get my book off the ground. I want to thank Andrea and my fellow New Camaldoli oblates and monks. You are my spiritual family, and I carry you in my heart.

You cannot forgive without grace, and grace is not
something you can demand. You can only sweep out
the chamber of your soul and be ready to receive it
when it comes.[1]

—Mirabai Starr

No matter how dark the tapestry God weaves for us,
there's always a thread of grace.[2]

—Mary Doria Russell

I did not plan on knitting a forgiveness prayer shawl or creating a
pattern of love and forgiveness. I believe God revealed both to me, and
He wants me to share my story and my pattern to encourage others.
That is why I wrote this book. It is my prayer that my story and
pattern will encourage and bless you on your journey to forgiveness.

It began when I was in my early twenties and pregnant with my
first child. I was happy and very excited about becoming a mother. I
never thought twice about my mother being there for me, and she was
there—for a few short months. I am grateful that my mother met her
first granddaughter and that she was there to help me learn some of
the basics of parenting. I guess we never think of losing our mothers,
especially when they are healthy and young, but my mother was taken
from me, suddenly and unexpectedly, when she was only forty-seven
years old. She was murdered. It was shocking. I was utterly and
completely devastated. There are no words that adequately describe
my painful, traumatic loss. As a psychotherapist for the past three
decades, I have met and worked with many people who have suffered

painful and traumatic losses and who also struggled to forgive. It is my experience and belief that we can only forgive life's big hurts through God's grace.

In this book, I tell my forgiveness story and share my faith journey to forgive the young man who murdered my mother. I share the beautiful ministry and amazing "miracle" visit that happened many years later and my simple, user-friendly love and forgiveness pattern. In the pattern, I knit together an ancient monastic prayer practice, *lectio divina*, with the art of knitting. You might be wondering, what is *lectio divina*? It means "divine reading."[3] It is an ancient practice of listening deeply to the voice of God speaking through sacred texts. It is a simple way of praying with scriptures or any sacred text.

First, read your chosen text very slowly and thoughtfully. Savor the words and listen for the "still, small voice" of a word or phrase that speaks to you and says, "I am the word for you today." Then ponder, taking the word or phrase into yourself by slowly repeating it and allowing it to interact with your inner world. Then begin to pray, interacting with God as you would with someone who loves and accepts you. I practice lectio divina in the morning, and I like to knit and pray with my word from scriptures. Anytime during the day that I pick up my needles, I remember my word in prayer.

The earliest Christian forms of lectio divina were practiced widely in the desert monastic tradition during the third to fifth centuries. The desert monks did not have their own Bibles, so they memorized large amounts of scripture, and they would meditate on the sacred texts as they went through the activities of their day.[4] As Saint Benedict taught, the monks listened for a word or phrase during their communal prayer and then held it in their hearts.[5] Christians have always seen a scriptural invitation *to* lectio divina in the example of the Virgin Mary's "pondering in her heart" what she saw and heard of Christ[6] (Luke 2:19).

I am certain you know about knitting, or maybe you know a knitter, or you have picked up knitting needles yourself. In my story, I share how knitting became my prayer practice and how, without conscious planning, I began knitting into the mystery of God, a forgiveness prayer shawl. It was this forgiveness prayer shawl, which I had not planned on knitting, that God chose for me to begin a ministry, honoring my mother and people who have lost a loved one through an act of violence. I began Dorothy's Peace and Forgiveness Prayer Shawl Ministry—but I am getting ahead of myself. You can read about this special ministry in chapter 3, "Forgiveness Prayer Shawl."

Knitting goes far back in world history. A sock was found in Egypt, thought to have been knitted in the third to fifth century. History believes knitting started in the Middle East and spread to Europe via trade routes. Knitted garments from the fourteenth century have been found in cathedral archives in Spain.[7] There are several paintings depicting the Virgin Mary knitting, one by Tommaso da Modena (circa 1325–1375) titled *Our Lady Knitting*.[8]

In her book *The Practice of Prayer* Margaret Guenther reminds us that the desert father, Abba Arsenius, gives three commands about prayer: "'Fuge!'Flee! Remove yourself physically to a quiet place, away from distractions, good and bad. 'Tace!' Be silent! Stop talking. 'Quiese!' Be inwardly still."[9] These prayer instructions are also good guidelines for practicing knitting or any handcraft as contemplative prayer.

In writing about my love and forgiveness pattern, I chose to use a basic prayer-shawl knitting pattern, but you can choose to knit, crochet, paint, sculpt, garden, carve wood, or do any craft you like that focuses on your hands doing the work. One participant in my forgiveness retreats said, "Oh, I can do this while I am doing my housework."

Having a desire to forgive, or perhaps feeling that you cannot forgive yet you want to have a desire to forgive, is all that is needed to use my simple pattern of love and forgiveness. In my pattern you will be guided to participate in spiritual exercises, titled "Practicing Forgiveness: Meditation, Journal Writing, Praying, and Knitting into God's Word," which is lectio divina. You can think of this pattern as a healing tool to add to your toolbox for your personal healing journey, through grieving to forgiveness.

In this book, when I use the word *lectio*, I am referring to the prayer practice *lectio divina* (see appendix B). All Bible quotes are taken from the Saint Joseph Edition of the New American Bible, 1986. When needed, names have been changed in my book to respect privacy.

× ×

PART ONE
A Forgiveness Journey

× ×

CHAPTER 1

Visits with Anna

When we forgive, we set a prisoner free and then
discover that the prisoner we set free was us.[1]
— Lewis B. Smedes

Wisdom teaches us that arriving at the Truth is
experiencing the graciousness and loving kindness
of God.[2]

— John Main

No one, least of all me, would have ever guessed what would
unfold after I signed on at my church's "Time and Talents
Weekend" to be a visitor to the sick and lonely. I thought there must
be something I could do to be of service as I strolled through my
church hall, looking at the various ministry options set up on the
tables. I saw the listing, "Visiting the Sick and Lonely," and thought,
"That's it. I could do that!" Never in a million years could I have
imagined what would come from that decision.

I first met Anna on a cold December day. I learned that Anna
had spent her career as a registered nurse in Queens, New York.
She had worked the entire time while raising her six children. Now
widowed and suddenly disabled, Anna had recently moved to central
Pennsylvania to live near her grown children. Life was not what she
expected it to be. She was a devout Catholic, now bedridden, and she
was unable to attend Mass.

I was given Anna's name as a person I could visit and bring

the Eucharist. What struck me most about Anna was her genuine concern for others, her sincere faith, and her cheerfulness. No matter what the circumstances, Anna's focus was always on the other person. I noticed her knitting projects as we talked about our common love of the art of knitting. Anna shared her prayer that she be allowed to continue to be of service and to bring joy to others. We could not have known how our lives were already connected.

On my second visit with Anna, I brought her a Christmas gift of yarn. Providentially, at that time I was starting a prayer shawl ministry at our church, so I invited Anna to join in by knitting prayer shawls. She was delighted. On my third visit to her home, while sitting with Anna, I noticed a beautiful prayer card on her table. Anna explained that her son was active in the prison ministry in our church and used the prayer on that card with the prisoners he visited. I told Anna that I had been invited to participate in the same prison ministry, but after much prayer and discernment, I'd declined. Wanting to explain, I said, "I have a fear of going into the men's prison because my mother was murdered." Anna lovingly replied, "Oh, of course, I understand." We continued our conversation and then Anna asked, "Where did your mother live?"

Hesitantly, I answered, "New York."

"Where in New York?" she asked.

I was becoming uncomfortable with the discussion, but I said, "Queens."

Then Anna asked, "Was the weather warm outside that day?"

"Yes," I said, "it was July."

"Had the murderer been in a hospital?"

"Yes."

"Did he sneak out his bedroom window?"

"Yes."

"Did your mother have red hair?"

"Yes."

At this point, I knew that she knew; and with tears in my eyes, I stood up feeling shock and disbelief. Light-headed and off balance, I could find no words for this moment. How could she possibly know? What were the chances of someone in central Pennsylvania knowing anything about this horrible murder that happened in Queens, New York, some thirty-nine years earlier? It was surreal—or maybe it was God.

Catching my breath, I sat back down. I remembered the day that I never wanted to think about again. In my mind I saw myself answering the telephone that hung on the kitchen wall. It was my father, asking, "Have you seen the newspaper?"

"No, why?" My heart was pounding. I knew something was wrong. My father had not spoken to me in months.

"Your mother was murdered last night," he said.

Without thinking, I asked, "Did you do it?"

With unusual calm, he said, "No, I did not."

I was not the only person to ask that question. My father had to answer to the police and to his attorney as to where he was when my mother was killed.

My parents recently had divorced and were in the middle of a custody battle. They had been immature high school sweethearts when they married at only eighteen and twenty years of age. They had four children and twenty-seven years of a violent, abusive marriage. When my mother and father divorced, she moved from her beautiful Long Island home into a small apartment in Queens that advertised twenty-four-hour security. At first, she had been excited. It was the first time in her adult life that she was making her own decisions. After years of being a stay-at-home mom, she loved her new sales job at Alexander's in New York City, but she felt very alone. She had no siblings and both her parents were deceased. Each evening, she had become accustomed to crossing the street in front of her apartment to a Chinese restaurant, where she would sit alone while nursing a Chivas Regal on ice. Then she would wobble back across the street. The security guard out front told me that he offered to help her, but she said, "No, thank you." I can see her walking with her head held high in her ladylike way as she walked with an unsteady gait toward her death. A seventeen-year-old boy, recently discharged to his parents' custody from a New York City psychiatric hospital, followed her into her building and into the same elevator. In front of her apartment door, he stabbed her many times and then dragged her into a nearby stairwell and raped her.

After hearing the details of my mother's death, I remember having no words, only intense emotions of anger, sadness, and fear. How was I supposed to go on? I felt guilty for being alive. I felt guilt for everything I did not do for my mother. I wished that I had spent more time with her, had had more patience with her, and had given her more love and attention. I just could not forgive myself. I wanted more time to love her and for her to get to know her grandchildren. Growing up in a violent home, I was always looking out for my mother, but this time I had not been able to protect her. Thankfully, Wayne, my only brother, three years my senior, and his new wife, Ronnie Sue, were flying in from California for mother's funeral. We were very close, and he was especially close to our mother, but even with Wayne there, I knew that from then on, I was going to feel completely abandoned. My mother was gone. I was in a state of shock and denial. I just managed to get through the motions of her funeral. My brother, sister-in-law, my husband, and I talked for hours. We stayed up till the wee hours while reminiscing about the happy times with our mother—how she loved to read and garden, how we would do the weeding while making up silly songs about weeds, how she loved to dance throughout the house while teaching us "Shuffle Off to Buffalo," and how she always baked our favorite chocolate cake with fudge icing and cooked my favorite, her chicken paprikash. Mom was strikingly beautiful, and we remembered that when she was eighteen years old and a dancer in a Broadway show, a Hollywood talent scout had picked her out from the chorus line and wanted to send her to Hollywood. At that time, my father said, "Let's get married." She said yes, and she did not continue her dancing career. When we got to the subject of her horrible death, we found ourselves blaming our father and ourselves. What could we have done differently? How might we have protected her? All too soon, it was time for my brother and his wife to fly back to California, for my husband to go back to work, and for me to focus on our new baby. Like my mother, I was a stay-at-home mom.

Reality started to hit when I went to her apartment to organize her belongings. The security guard, working the night my mother was killed, came over to me and shared his condolences. I thanked him for trying to help and continued into my mother's building. I felt that I was walking in her footsteps. Her presence was all around me. I stepped onto the elevator and pictured her on this same elevator with the young man who killed her. As I stepped off the elevator and walked in the hallway toward her apartment, I saw the blood stains on the walls around her apartment door. In my mind, I was reliving her death, and tears flowed copiously as I went inside her apartment and collapsed with the sheer agony of it all. I stayed in the apartment for many hours. I cleaned and sorted her things, and I even tried to clean the hallway walls, stained with her blood. Maybe I was trying to wash away what happened, make it somehow less awful. Then I went to the police station to pick up my mother's belongings. They handed me her purse, her ring with blood still visible in its crevices, and one lone, dangling earring. I thanked the officer and walked outside in a fog, even though the sun was shining, as I hailed a taxi. A couple of weeks later, without thinking, I picked up the phone on the wall in my kitchen to call my mother and suddenly remembered that she would not be answering. She had died. I could never again call her or hear her voice. I was a twenty-three-year-old new mother, very much in need of my mom's love and guidance. I broke down and sobbed as the painful reality set in, and I felt as if my heart was breaking.

"I remember the day," Anna shared. "We were driving home when we heard on the news about the murder, and we thought that he might have killed a red-haired woman in our apartment building." She continued, "The name of that young man is Russell. I knew him and his family, because we lived in the same apartment building. My children went to school with him. His family was lovely and well respected, but he was troubled." I was still speechless as Anna continued, "His mother shared with me that one night she awoke to see her son, standing over her, holding a knife over her head. She tried to get help for him. The night he committed the murder, he had sneaked out a window without her knowing that he was gone. The next morning, she found his bloody clothes and shoes. She knew that she had to contact the police, and she did."

In that instant I felt deep compassion for this mother and her son. For her, because she had to turn in her own child; and for him, because he was a victim of his own mental illness. This graced moment of compassion filled me with a palpable awareness of God's presence. I knew that this meeting with Anna was clearly orchestrated by God. It was a "miracle." Finally, I found some words to speak.

"Anna, you have no idea what a blessing this is. All these years, I have had many unanswered questions about my mother's death. It never made any sense to me. For years, I was convinced that my father had somehow been a part of planning her death because at that time, my parents were in a difficult custody battle, following an equally nasty and difficult divorce. The timing of her death always seemed too convenient. I struggled with survivor guilt and wished I could have protected her. All we knew at the time was that a seventeen-year-old boy, who had been in a psychiatric hospital, had committed the murder. I lived in Brooklyn, New York, and my mother had recently moved to Queens, New York. I continued to look out for my mother as much as possible, while taking care of my new baby. We would mostly talk on the phone and sometimes enjoy a visit together. I could not imagine what went on in the seventeen-year-old's mind to cause him to commit murder. To kill my mother! My life would never be the same again. I felt the depth of despair. I felt depressed, angry, and lost. I had failed to keep my mother safe, and I blamed myself for years. I also blamed my father. Even if he had not actually arranged her death, his violence toward her was a part of her being unsafe and killed. She would not have been living alone in an apartment. My world, as I knew it growing up, was defined by my efforts to protect my mother from my father's violence. I imagined that Russell's mother also lived a life trying to protect her son and others from his mental illness. She, like me, had tried and failed."

Anna said, "Cheryl, I can tell you absolutely, beyond a shadow of a doubt, that your mother was not murdered by any arrangement. I knew Russell's family, and they were outstanding citizens of the community who were greatly respected. The boy was seriously disturbed." Then Anna shared many more details about Queens, my mother's neighborhood, Russell and his family, their apartment building, and other neighbors in the building. After listening to Anna, I felt that after thirty-nine years, I finally knew what had happened to my mother. It was thirty-nine years of prayer, seeking God, and wanting to forgive that prepared me to receive God's gift of compassion. I felt it for Russell and his mother. This graced moment in time was a miracle. In God's timing, I received the grace to forgive. There was a shift within my heart, a transformation. I felt forgiveness deep inside me for young Russell. His mental illness was to blame, not him. Knowing about the real people involved, even their names, helped, but I know it was through God's grace that I could forgive.

Finally, after some thirty-nine years, I was able to put my mother's murder and my suspicions about her death to rest and to feel peace. At the end of this visit, I reached over and held Anna's hand and looked into her eyes. I said, "Anna, you don't ever have to wonder whether you are going to be of service. Look at how God has used you today to bring my mother's story home to me. You have brought the greatest healing and joy to my life today."

Anna nodded and smiled wisely.

Spending some time with Anna

CHAPTER 2

Forgiveness: A Path to Love

God is love, and whoever remains in love remains in God and God in him.

—1 John 4:16–21

If we have no peace, it is because we have forgotten that we belong to each other.[1]

—Mother Teresa

When I arrived home after my visit with Anna, I wondered, "What brought me to visit Anna? Why was I able to feel compassion for Russell and his mother now and to forgive Russell after all of these years?" I took out my trusty journal, a spiral-bound notebook, and started writing. I remembered that following my mother's death, I was literally a brand-new baptized Christian Catholic of eight months. I came from a Jewish background. Though my mother had been raised a Catholic, she had converted to Judaism when she married, and we children had been raised in the Reform Jewish faith. I remembered attending services at our temple on the high holy days: Rosh Hashanah and Yom Kippur (the Day of Atonement), when we would ask God for forgiveness for any and all of our sins for the year. Looking back, it made sense that when I would come to know and believe in Jesus Christ as the Messiah, it would be through the prophet Isaiah.

As I wrote in my journal, I remembered that special time. I was twenty-three years old, Jewish, pregnant with my first child, and married to my Catholic husband. I wondered what religion we would put on our child's birth certificate. My friend at the bank, where I was employed, gave me the name of a Catholic priest to visit. I started to see him weekly. The priest, knowing that I was Jewish, took out his Bible and opened it on his desk. I sat beside him as we read through the book of Isaiah. It was a beautiful time for me as I read the words of Isaiah, and we discussed what they meant. One day as we were reading, I became acutely aware that Isaiah's words were about the Messiah and that they were describing Jesus Christ. Christ, in ancient Greek, means "anointed" and is a translation of the Hebrew, the Messiah.[2] The words entered my heart. Later, I learned that that moment was an epiphany, a manifestation of God. Some of the lines that enlightened me were the following:

> Who would believe what we have heard?
> To whom has the arm of the Lord been revealed?
> He grew up like a sapling before him,
> Like a shoot from the parched earth;
> There was in him no stately bearing
> to Make us look at him,
> Nor appearance that would attract us To him.
> He was spurned and avoided by men
> A man of suffering, accustomed to infirmity,
> One of those from whom men hide their faces,
> Spurned, and we held him in no esteem.
> Yet it was our infirmities that he bore,
> Our sufferings that he endured,
> While we thought of him as stricken,
> As one smitten by God and afflicted.
> But he was pierced for our offenses,
> Crushed for our sins,
> Upon him was the chastisement that
> Makes us whole,
> By his stripes we were healed.

We had all gone astray like sheep,
Each following his own way;
But the Lord laid upon him the guilt of us all.
Though he was harshly treated,
He submitted and opened not his mouth;
Like a lamb led to the slaughter
Or a sheep before the Shearers,
He was silent and opened not his mouth.

—Isaiah 53:1–7

"If he gives his life as an offering for Sin, He shall see his descendants in a long Life, And the will of the Lord shall be accomplished Through him" (Isaiah 53:10).

When I learned that Jesus, His parents, and all of the apostles except Luke were Jewish, I felt a connection between my Jewish roots and my new Judeo-Christian faith. I was baptized and married in the Catholic Church. A few weeks later, I gave birth to my first child, a beautiful baby girl. It was shortly after I was blessed with the gift of motherhood that I lost my mother. This was the beginning of my Christian journey, and I knew that to follow Jesus Christ required living His radical message of love and forgiveness. I had received God's forgiveness in my baptism, in the sacrament of reconciliation, and each time I received Him in the Eucharist at Mass, but how could I forgive the horrific murder of my mother? Grief had stripped me raw to the bone. I felt that my heart was permanently broken. The author Mirabai Starr, who suffered the tragic loss of a child, said, "As we cry out in the anguish of our loss, the boundless love of God comes pouring into the shattered container of our hearts. The refilling of our emptiness is a mystery, it is grace, and it is built into the human condition."[3]

I opened my New Testament for guidance. I read, "If you forgive others their transgressions, your heavenly Father will forgive you. But if you do not forgive others, neither will your Father forgive your transgressions" (Matthew 6:14–15).

It was clear to me, intellectually, that I needed to forgive, but could I? The last meal Jesus would share with His apostles was the Passover Seder. It was during this meal that Jesus said, "I give you a new commandment: love one another. As I have loved you, so you should love one another. This is how all will know you are my disciples, if you have love for one another" (John 13:34–35).

As I continued to write in my journal and look back, I realized how integral my inner healing and faith had been to my forgiveness process. The loss of my mother brought home to me Christ's radical and challenging gospel message: "You shall love the Lord your God with all your heart, with all your soul, with all your mind, and with all your strength. The second is this: You shall love your neighbor as yourself. There is no other commandment greater than these" (Mark 12:30–31).

This was a tall order for someone coming out of an angry, abusive childhood, where I was judged harshly. I had to change my early childhood beliefs and learn to let go of self-condemnation and the condemnation of others. I had to learn how to love. I remembered going through the five stages of grieving, as Dr. Elisabeth Kubler-Ross describes in her book *On Grief and Grieving*: denial, anger, depression, bargaining, and acceptance.[4] I bounced back and forth, up and down, as I went through the stages of the grieving process, journaling and praying all the way. At times, I pounded the doors of heaven with my anger and grief. I also found Dennis and Matthew Linn's book *Healing Life's Hurts* very helpful, as it guided me through healing my memories and sharing all of my feelings with Christ.[5] I finally did reach the fifth stage of acceptance, although I did not understand why my mother had been killed, and I continued to carry my suspicions that my father had been responsible for her death.

My Judeo-Christian faith assured me that I would see my mother one day, and this belief brought me great comfort, but for many years I carried around much unhealed trauma and pain from my childhood. Without my realizing it, this extra baggage was blocking me from fully experiencing God's love and forgiveness.

I knew intellectually that God's love and forgiveness were unconditional, but I did not feel loved or forgiven. How could I give that which I felt I had not received? I prayed, read scriptures, wrote in my journal, was active in my church, and attended Mass regularly. It was during those early years after my mother's death that my Jewish paternal grandmother taught me how to knit. She would knit beautiful afghans, while I knitted baby items for my children, such as blankets, bunting, and ponchos. This was the beginning of my love of knitting. One day, those stitches would be accompanied by prayers.

I loved reading books about my faith. One of my favorite authors was Thomas Merton, a Trappist monk. His world-famous book *The Seven Storey Mountain*, the autobiography of his faith journey, from barely knowing God to his conversion to Catholicism, first attracted me to contemplative prayer. He became a Trappist monk, committed to a life of prayer and silence. He became the most prolific and sought-after Catholic writer of the twentieth century. Merton once was asked, "What is grace?" His answer: "It is God's own life, shared by us. God's life is Love."[6] To this day, I continue to read and enjoy books by Merton. Another of the many authors I enjoyed was Catherine de Hueck Doherty and her book *Poustinia*. She wrote about silence, the desert, and prayer. I read *Poustinia* straight through in one night. She describes the poustinia as a state of being constantly in the presence of God, a state that is within all of us, within our hearts.[7] I believe that sitting with God in silent prayer was a large part of my healing. Only in silence can we hear the voice of God, and it was in silence that God chipped away at my defenses, pulling me toward Him. Little by little, over the years, I cleared a path within, making room for God, room to receive His gift of love and forgiveness. This was a slow healing process that evolved over many years. During those years, I met with my spiritual director, Sister Jeanne-Marie. This spiritual direction felt as if I were hiking around a mountain on the same trail, many times over, but it was through this inner spiritual and psychological process of going deeper and deeper, with a trusted spiritual companion, that I found healing, I could feel God's love and forgiveness. Years later,

I knew that my own positive healing experience through spiritual direction was what inspired me to become a spiritual director, certified in contemplative spiritual direction.

As I continued to read my Bible, two stories appealed to me in particular—that of the Prodigal Son and that of the woman caught in adultery. Both spoke to me of how much God loves and forgives us. I learned from these Bible stories, that forgiveness is a path to love.

The parable of the prodigal son is about a man who had two sons, and the younger son asked his father for and received his early inheritance. He left home and squandered it all. When a severe famine struck, he found himself without food. After coming to his senses, he realized that his father's hired workers had more than enough to eat, while he was starving. He decided to go home. While he was still a long way off, his father caught sight of him and was filled with compassion. He ran to his son and embraced him and kissed him.

His son said to him, "'Father, I have sinned against heaven and against you; I no longer deserve to be called your son.' But his father ordered his servants, 'Quickly bring the finest robe and put it on him; put a ring on his finger and sandals on his feet. Take the fattened calf and slaughter it. Then let us celebrate with a feast, because this son of mine was dead, and has come to life again; he was lost, and has been found.' Then the celebration began" (Luke 15:20–24).

The story of the woman caught in adultery occurred while Jesus was teaching in the temple. There was suddenly a commotion as a group of scribes and Pharisees dragged a woman toward him. They said, "Teacher, this woman was caught in the very act of committing adultery. In the Law, Moses commanded us to stone such women. What do you say?" They said this to test Him. Jesus was silent. Bending down, He began writing on the ground. The group of Pharisees and scribes demanded a reply. "What do you say?" Jesus stood up and said to them, "Let the one without sin, throw the first stone." Again, He bent down and wrote with His finger on the ground. The men started to leave, one by one, beginning with the eldest. (It was the tradition for the eldest to throw the first stone.)

"Then Jesus straightened up and said to her, 'Woman, where are they? Has no one condemned you?' She replied, 'No one, sir.' Then Jesus said, 'Neither do I condemn you. Go, and from now on do not sin any more'" (John 8:4–11).

These two stories touched me deeply. I could feel myself waiting for the stones that never came, and I was there, expecting to eat with the hired hands. I was and I am vividly aware of how our God of love unconditionally forgives us when we make big mistakes, and He welcomes us with a feast fit for a king when we are broken and hungry, and we find our way home.

I remembered that in the early years of my Catholic faith, I was drawn to Mother Teresa and her work with the poor. I still am. Her life and her devotion to Christ—and the way that she saw Him in the distressing disguise of the poor—deeply molded my faith. While I was rearing my three daughters, I was a Saint Vincent de Paul volunteer home visitor, and I would always take one of my daughters with me on my visits to the poverty-stricken families in our town. While talking with my youngest daughter recently, she reminded me of some of my life experiences that prepared and led me to visit with Anna.

She said, "It was because you always visited with people in need as a Saint Vincent de Paul volunteer. I remember sitting with you in a house that had nothing on the floor but one mattress. After we left the house, you said, 'I gave that family a voucher for the thrift store to receive, without cost, a sofa, bed, kitchen table, refrigerator, and clothing, but what I received was much more valuable. In my mind, I had just visited with Jesus.'"

My daughter also said, "Mom, you spent your life as a therapist, sitting with people in their need. I think that is also why you visited with Anna. It's what you do, and God rewarded you with information about your mother's death." I believe that God put the desire in my heart to help the poor, and, as Mother Teresa described, when I visited a family in poverty, I felt His presence. To this day, when I sit with my therapy clients, my office feels like holy ground.

Looking back, I could see God's thread of unconditional love knitted throughout my grieving, healing, and forgiveness process. Slowly, I grew to accept my mother's murder and to accept myself. I discovered my pride had not allowed God to be God while I was stuck in the quicksand of self-blame. As the years went by and I became less stuck, I became more open to God. My faith was growing, and I began to see all people, including Russell, as children of God. The violence that he committed against my family did not make him less forgiven by God, yet what he did was evil, and his actions had consequences. Russell was in prison for twenty-three years. I saw how my faith in God guided my forgiveness journey and how in God's timing, He brought Anna and me together, and I received, through His grace, the gift of compassion and forgiveness.

CHAPTER 3

Forgiveness Prayer Shawl

You formed my inmost being; you knit me in my
mother's womb.

—Psalm 139:13

A prayer shawl is intended to be a reminder of God's
ever-present love. It is as near to you as your own
body is to your spirit.[1]

—Jeannette Bakke, Lois Lindbloom

I continued to write in my journal. I could see the synchronicity
in how I came to knit a forgiveness prayer shawl shortly before
meeting Anna. A few years earlier, two of my daughters had a
misunderstanding, and one of them decided that she needed some
time away from the family. Shortly before this happened, I had
enjoyed a visit with these two lovely daughters. One afternoon, while
shopping, we stopped in a small yarn shop. I asked my daughters
to choose a pattern and some yarn and told them that I would knit
something for each one. A couple of months later, after one daughter
had gone on her sabbatical, I found the yarn and pattern for the shawl
that she had chosen. I started to knit each evening after work. I would
knit and pray, usually in silence. From that silence, prayers flowed
from somewhere deep within my heart. I was praying for each of my
three daughters and for reconciliation within our family.

As I knitted and worked the pattern, I started to feel better—
closer to my daughter since she left for her sabbatical from everyone in

our immediate family. I couldn't talk to her, but I could knit something especially for her. I felt close to her as I knitted and prayed. The shawl took several months to complete, with many rip-outs and much needed guidance from my local Stitch Your Art Out Yarn Shop. The months went by; and as I continued to respect my daughter's need for space, I kept knitting and praying.

I had been practicing meditation for more than three decades, and I had discovered that just as in silent, contemplative prayer, when I am knitting and praying, I enter into God's presence. The heart of the person I am praying for feels as if it is touching my heart. In *The Knitting Sutra*, Susan Gordon Lydon writes, "The very rhythm of the knitting needles can become as incantatory as a drumbeat or Gregorian chant."[2]

I did not know about the prayer shawl ministry when I started on my journey of praying and knitting. It happened quite by accident but of course, there are no accidents with God. As my needles moved across each row, one stitch at a time, I experienced a deep inner quieting and healing, while praying prayers of love and forgiveness. It became my knitting meditation. I was intuitively aware that God was working through my prayers as I knitted. During this time, I read an article "Knitting into the Mystery of God" by Susan Izard in the magazine *Presence: An International Journal of Spiritual Direction*.[3] I knew immediately that I had had that experience. I began to read about the national prayer shawl ministry. I felt that I had found the meaning behind my own knitting and prayer.

The prayer shawl ministry was begun in May 1997 by two women: Janet Bristow and Victoria A. Cole-Galo. They were graduating from the Women's Leadership Institute at the Hartford Seminary in Hartford, Connecticut. A member in their class asked them to pray with her for her ill husband. The lady wrapped herself in her brightly colored shawl and as they joined hands in prayer, it was clear to Victoria and Janet that every time she wore this shawl, she felt their love and support. The next time Victoria and Janet saw this shawl, it was the altar cloth at the woman's husband's funeral service. This symbol of a shawl was powerful to them, because they knew that the shawl would always be a comfort and symbol of prayer.

Victoria and Janet both felt drawn to the shawl image, symbolic of the comforting, motherly, unconditional love of God. As these two women continued to knit and pray, they realized their handwork was becoming their spiritual practice. They were eager to share their experience and give gifts of shawls to family and friends, and as they did, needs for shawls grew—and a ministry was born! This was the beginning of the worldwide prayer shawl ministry.[4] One can find more information, stories, prayers, and shawl patterns at the website: www.shawlministry.com.

When my shawl was finished, I brought it to my church prayer group and asked them if they thought anyone in our church would be interested in forming a prayer shawl group. Admiring my shawl, they said yes and told me to put an ad in our bulletin. One lady, Marge, experienced in the art of crocheting and a faithful member of our church, said with a smile, "I want to be there when you start." That is how Marge and I began our church prayer shawl ministry. We met weekly on Tuesday mornings and once a month on Saturday mornings. We had about fourteen women knitting and crocheting prayer shawls, six of them regulars.

About three weeks after my first prayer shawl was completed, my daughter called and said, "How are you, Mom? I have missed you." I was thrilled. When I visited with my daughter, I presented her with the shawl, and she loved it. After reading the prayer-shawl card, she said, "That's how you always sign your letters, Mom: 'with love and prayers.'" As she wrapped it around her shoulders, I too felt wrapped in prayers. I had not planned or even thought through what had developed. I realized only after it was done that this shawl was a forgiveness prayer shawl. Each stitch was filled with prayers for reconciliation within our family.

Anna and I continued our weekly visits. During one of them, while bringing yarn to Anna, I had a deep, intuitive feeling that I wanted to knit a forgiveness shawl for Russell's mother. I asked Anna what she thought of this idea. She nodded with certainty and said, "That's God!" We both understood. I said to Anna, "Even if I never meet Russell's mother, I will knit this shawl in honor of her. It will be filled with prayers of forgiveness." I never did meet Russell's mother, in spite of trying my best to find her, but I did knit a prayer shawl in her honor, and I gave it to a mother who had lost her child through an act of violence. This was the real beginning of the ministry to honor my mother, Dorothy, and families who have lost a loved one through an act of violence. We called it Dorothy's Peace and Forgiveness Prayer Shawl Ministry, though I didn't know it at the time.

One day, after much thought, I felt inspired to share with Marge my experience with Anna to see what she thought about including families victimized by acts of violence in our prayer shawl ministry. Marge agreed that we should do this. We had no sooner decided to pursue the idea than a local murder occurred. We gathered to see if we could get in touch with this family. We were wondering how to deliver a shawl respectfully when Marge's phone rang. It was her friend Rose. Marge told Rose about our trying to find a way to deliver a prayer shawl to this family. Rose said that she knew the daughter of the victim. They had worked together, and Rose would be happy to pick up the shawl and deliver it to the daughter. Marge and I both had goose bumps and felt that it was a sign from God to go forward with our idea to give prayer shawls to families who had been victimized by acts of violence and murder.

I told Marge, "I want a special prayer card to honor my mother and other families victimized by violence, to go along with our regular prayer card and shawl."

Marge said, "Cheryl, you had better go home right now and create that prayer card, because Rose will be picking up the shawl tomorrow."

Now, I am not a computer-savvy person, so I consider what happened a blessing from God. I was able to create a perfectly beautiful prayer card using the peace prayer of Saint Francis. At our next prayer shawl meeting, Marge and I shared this beautiful story, and with the group's blessing, in honor of my mother, Dorothy, we officially added Dorothy's Peace and Forgiveness Prayer Shawls as a "wing" to our ministry.

Our prayer shawl ministry decided also to donate shawls to our local domestic violence shelter for women and children. We included Dorothy's Peace and Forgiveness Prayer Card with each shawl. Our ministry grew as murders occurred in surrounding towns. We decided to cover the geographic area in our church diocese and have volunteers in each area. We called the volunteers when we needed a shawl delivered in their area. To respect the family's privacy, we delivered our prayer shawls to the funeral home or, if known, to their faith community. Dorothy's Peace and Forgiveness Prayer Shawl Ministry continues today in central Pennsylvania, under the kind direction of Sister Jeanne-Marie.

Here are a few of the people who received shawls from our Dorothy's Peace and Forgiveness Prayer Shawl Ministry: I remember the red, white, and blue shawl given to the mother of an eighteen-year-old son and brother who died in the Iraq war. We were blessed when we gave a shawl to the sister of a young man who tragically murdered their mother. We gave a prayer shawl to a mother who lost her naval officer son while he was walking with his fiancée and was gunned down. We gave prayer shawls to a grandmother and three grandchildren whose mother had been shot. A prayer shawl was humbly given to the mother of a young man killed while on duty with a border patrol. These are only a few examples when prayer shawls brought comfort to families during the excruciating pain of losing a loved one through an act of violence.

Giving a shawl to someone grieving can be difficult, especially because you do not know what the recipient's reaction will be. You know that your gift cannot take away the pain, but be assured that every prayer shawl is a concrete expression of God's love. When we give prayer shawls to people who have lost loved ones, they always thank us and share how much their shawl comforts them and how they can feel God's love when wrapped in it. We too feel blessed and can sense His presence as we knit in prayer for each person who will receive a prayer shawl. The author Susan Gordon Lydon writes: "The important thing is not so much what you knit as what happens to you while you are knitting, where the interior journey takes you."[5]

When we experience a loss, there is usually a component of forgiveness. Sometimes we need to forgive ourselves, as I did, for the things we feel we did not do for our loved one. We also have to forgive the person who left us, by illness or violence. We actually have to forgive God at times, because it is natural to blame him for our losses, and of course there are many reasons we need to forgive. These could be a spouse seeking a divorce, a family member relocating far away, children leaving home and not visiting very often, losing a job, a friend not being there for us, and the list goes on. Forgiveness is a part of grieving and a natural consequence of life. The most difficult person to forgive, I believe, is oneself. We can easily become stuck, thinking negative thoughts about ourselves because of our not forgiving ourselves. In my pattern of love and forgiveness I found a simple way to forgive through knitting and praying.

Here are a few of the many ways our Pennsylvania Prayer Shawl Ministry, through knitted prayer shawls, has touched lives. A prayer shawl was given to an eighty-year-old volunteer at our local Pennsylvania University when she was ill and in the hospital. She shared that the prayer shawl helped her to get better. She did recover and wears her shawl everywhere, even when volunteering, and she tells everyone about her prayer shawl. A Catholic man requested a prayer shawl for his Muslim mother, who lived in Holland. Our Pennsylvania Prayer Shawl Ministry sent a prayer shawl to his mother. She was buried with it wrapped around her shoulders. Lisa, a daughter of Marge, worked with a lady who was depressed. Her sister had passed away that summer, and her other sister was in the hospital with stage four cancer. Lisa asked her if she would like a prayer shawl. She said, "You can give my sister a prayer shawl, but she doesn't believe in anything anymore." When her sister received the shawl, she said that she immediately started to feel better. Then her doctor told her that her chemotherapy did not work, and he sent her home to live with her children. After a few weeks, she felt much better and returned to her own home. When she returned to her doctor, he told her she was cancer-free. Miracles do happen.

A few years ago, I moved to California in order to be near my adult children and precious grandsons. I was very happy to be invited to organize a prayer shawl ministry at my new church. We give prayer shawls to people in need, and each Christmas, we give prayer shawls to a domestic violence shelter, serving women and children. At Christmas, we also give, through the Office of Restorative Justice, two forgiveness prayer shawls for two mothers who have lost a loved one to violence. With each shawl, we include our regular prayer shawl card and Dorothy's Peace and Forgiveness Prayer Card.

In the Pennsylvania and in the California prayer shawl ministries, I experienced a community of women who love God, prayer, knitting and crocheting, and a desire to bring the love of God to people through a handmade and prayed-over shawl. It is an amazing ministry. The most common reason we give a prayer shawl to someone is because the person has experienced a loss.

Here are a few of the many stories from our California Prayer Shawl Ministry. I remember when our prayer shawl ministry sent a shawl to the ailing brother of a parishioner living in London, England. He loved his shawl, and when he passed away, his wife found that her husband's prayer shawl gave her great comfort during her grieving. One of our devoted prayer shawl members, Anne, volunteered at a domestic violence shelter and spent time with a child. She had this beautiful child help her choose the yarn and pattern for a prayer shawl that she knitted for the shelter's yearly fund-raiser. The shawl was absolutely exquisite. The colors were yellow and mango. Ann found that she needed to move back home to Ohio for her employment. I chose the same yarn in the same colors, yellow and mango, thinking that it would be a loving reminder of our shawl group and her special relationship with the little girl. It was her going-away prayer shawl gift. Ann was stunned and often writes to let us know how much her shawl comforts her and keeps her warm. One day Ann contacted me and requested a shawl for her dear friend, Susan, who had just lost her husband. I sent the shawl, and Ann let me know that Susan attended First Friday Mass with some couples, as she and her husband had done for many years. She had just returned home to experience her First Friday without him. She was feeling very low, and then the doorbell rang. It was the delivery of our prayer shawl. Susan's spirits soared, and she felt comforted. Susan later wrote and thanked us for her shawl. She shared that she reads the prayer card with the shawl often and said that she is humbled by its effect on her. She plans to wrap her family in it when her grown kids come to visit for Christmas, and Susan said, "It will be our new tradition." Susan was to experience her first winter alone. She said in her note, "I promise you, I will reach for my shawl to remind me I am loved."

Prayer Shawl

A Knitting Prayer
May this shawl filled with prayers
Always be a comfort, and
Surround the wearer with
God's healing presence, love, and hope.
Amen

Directions:

A basic knitting prayer-shawl pattern, filled with prayers of forgiveness for or in honor of a person or group (adapted from the basic prayer shawl pattern by Victoria A. Cole-Galo and Janet Bristow, on their website, www.shawlministry.com).[6]

Supplies:

- 6 skeins of medium worsted weight yarn of choice
- one pair of straight or circular knitting needles, size 11
- a journal
- pen
- a sacred text

Choose a sacred text from the Bible and/or spiritual reading.

Finished size: approximately 18–24 inches wide by 53–60 inches or desired length.

Directions: Cast on 54 (57, 60) stitches.

Garter stitch pattern: Knit each stitch across the first row, repeat this row until the shawl is the desired length. Bind off all stitches across last row, cut yarn, and knot. Weave in loose threads.

Fringe: Cut yarn in lengths twice the length you desire for fringe. For example, for a 6-inch fringe, cut 12-inch lengths. I cut a cardboard square about 6 inches square and wrap my yarn around it several times. Then I cut the yarn straight across the top of the cardboard. It gives me 12-inch strands. Usually I cut enough for six 12-inch strands of fringe for every few stitches across the width of the shawl. Fold a few strands of cut yarn in half, insert crochet hook into a stitch on either the cast-on row or bound-off edge. Pull up loops by catching the length of fringe at its center point, and pull the loose ends through the loop. Pull tight.

CHAPTER 4

Prayers from the Heart

Forgiveness has the power to heal both our inner and outer lives.[1]

—Gerald Jampolsky, MD

As far as the east is from the west, God removes our transgressions from us.

—Psalm 103

One day, while I was writing in my journal about forgiveness, five words appeared on the journal page: remembering, gathering, holding, gleaning, and transformation. I had not thought about them. They just appeared. I knew the words alone were not prayers, but intuitively, I felt they were important and could somehow guide my inner healing and lead me into prayer. Over several months and much knitting, praying, and journal writing, the meaning for each word eventually became clear. I was on a quest to discover what I was supposed to do with these prayer words. I continued to knit and pray, and one day God revealed that these five words were prayers from the heart: *a pattern of love and forgiveness.* The Russian Orthodox bishop Theophan said, "Pray with the mind in your heart."[2] That is what happens when you practice with my pattern of love and forgiveness. You are praying with your mind and prayers from the heart. *Remembering* is about recalling what hurt us so that we can forgive with God's grace. *Gathering* is about collecting our thoughts, feelings, and memories and writing them in our journal. *Holding* is about our journal and how it safely keeps all of our words, just as God's love holds us. *Gleaning* is about knitting into God's Word—lectio divina—and gleaning His Word that speaks to our hearts. *Transformation* is what happens when knitting and praying in God's presence; when slowly, in God's timing, our hearts are healed and our lives are transformed by His love. As I contemplated these words, I saw my life. I thought, *I have always written in my journal.* I remembered writing and expressing my deepest emotions in my journal after my mother died. It was a large part of my grief process. Gleaning came naturally for me as a Camaldolese oblate, with my daily practice of lectio. In the morning, while sipping hot tea, I wrapped myself in my old, frayed prayer shawl, sat down in my worn prayer chair, and began to read the daily scriptures, slowly, reverentially listening for the word that was meant for me. I picked up my needles and started to knit and meditate on my word. It made perfect sense to remember my hurt and desire to forgive while meditating on God's Word. I was blessed. I felt that God gave me a simple way, a Benedictine way, to stay close to Him and to forgive. I was knitting and praying with His Word, lectio divina. It is there in His Word that we can personally meet God and receive His love and forgiveness. Forgiveness begins first by receiving God's love and forgiveness within ourselves. God's love opens our hearts, and with an open heart and in His timing, we receive His grace to forgive.

The simplicity of this pattern and the use of my hands while knitting and praying reminded me of a knitting retreat I attended with my Pennsylvania prayer shawl group at a Benedictine monastery in upstate New York. It was there that I started to recognize the first seeds of my call to become a Benedictine oblate. As John Chryssavgis said in his book *In the Heart of the Desert*, "Theirs is a silence of the deep heart and of intense prayer, a silence that cuts through centuries and cultures. We should stop to hear that heartbeat."[3] I first heard that heartbeat while visiting the New York Benedictine monks, and it left an imprint on my heart. Two years later, after my move to California, I learned from my dear friend Barbara about the monks at

New Camaldoli Hermitage in Big Sur, California. My heart stirred, because I knew Big Sur in earlier years from visiting with my brother, who lived there. I thought this might be a sign, and after much prayer, I started a twelve-month period of prayer and discernment to decide if God was calling me to become a New Camaldoli Benedictine oblate. The oblate is a layperson joined in spiritual vows to support the monks of New Camaldoli, in bonds of friendship and prayer.[4]

It was during those months of study and prayer that I learned and began to practice the ancient monastic prayer practice of lectio divina, praying with scriptures. In my reading, I discovered that the ancient practice of lectio has its roots in Judaism. These roots can be found in the Hebrew method of studying scripture, called *haga*, a process of learning by heart.[5] Haga was part of the devotional practice of the Jews in the days of Jesus. The Jews would memorize the text in a process that involved repeating the passage over and over softly with the lips, until the words themselves gradually took up residence in the heart, thereby transforming the person's life. This touched me deeply and was affirming to me on October 23, 2011, as I took my vows and became a New Camaldoli oblate. I included knitting in my practice of lectio, and as I knitted prayed, and repeated the scriptures, I felt and still feel God drawing me closer. My faith and relationship to Him grew stronger each day. I believe practicing my pattern of love and forgiveness deepened my love for God and transformed my heart through His love and forgiveness. As the Buddhists say, "Enlightenment may be achieved through the repetition of sutra, or prayer: Pattern also is formed by repetition; its beauty deepens and grows each time it is repeated."[6]

x x x x x x x x x x x x x x x x x x x x x x x x x x x x x x x

PART TWO
A Pattern of Love and Forgiveness

x x x x x x x x x x x x x x x x x x x x x x x x x x x x x x x

The following five chapters present my simple pattern of love and forgiveness—prayers from the heart. Each chapter opens with the meaning of one prayer from the heart, and each chapter includes the spiritual exercises titled Practicing Forgiveness: Silent Meditation, Journal Writing, Scripture, and Knitting into God's Word—Lectio Divina.

Before we delve more deeply into the pattern, try this simple lectio exercise:

Write out a simple verse that you like from scriptures. Now, read it very slowly and contemplatively, "listening with the ear of your heart," as Saint Benedict taught in the prologue of his Rule[7], until one word speaks to your heart. That is your word from God. Take some time to meditate on your word. When you are ready, pick up your needles and start to knit or start the craft of your choice, and pray.

CHAPTER 5

Remembering: The Person or Group You Want to Forgive

He has remembered His covenant forever.
—Psalm 105:8

The only way to get over the resentment for the remembered wrong is to forgive.[1]
—Lewis B. Smedes

The Hebrew word for "remember" is *zakar*. In the Old Testament, *zakar* is often used in expressions about God's "remembering" His covenant with His people.[2] For example, in Exodus 2:24, it says: "God heard their groaning, and God remembered His Covenant with Abraham, with Isaac, and with Jacob." In this example, God's remembering His covenant leads to His active intervention to rescue Israel from slavery. All of the ways *zakar* is used in the Old and New Testaments involves a knowledge accompanied by an action.

In the New Testament, Jesus on the night He was handed over, took bread, and after He had given thanks, broke it and said, "This is my body that is for you. Do this in remembrance of me." In the same way also the cup, after supper, saying, "This cup is the New Covenant in my blood. Do this, as often as you drink it, in remembrance of me" (1 Corinthians 11:24–25).

When we remember our life experiences, some may cause us joy while others may cause us pain. If we desire to forgive someone or a group who has hurt us, my experience teaches that we need God's Grace to forgive. In my pattern of love and forgiveness, we lift up to God our joy, our hurt, and our desire to forgive, as we meditate on God's Word.

We too can follow our remembering with action as we lift up our knitting needles and yarn in prayer. God loves and forgives us unconditionally, no matter what we have done. When we open our hearts and receive His love and forgiveness through His grace, we can forgive ourselves and others. When we knit a forgiveness prayer shawl, we are knitting in prayer for someone, or in honor of someone, or for a group that has hurt us that we want to forgive or at least have the desire to forgive. When we are remembering the recipient of our shawl with prayers, we too are being healed. Prayer changes us. Knitting in prayer is both knowledge and action.

Sometimes it is only with a thread of grace that we begin our journey to forgiveness. Slowly, in God's time and through perseverance in prayer, the thread becomes stronger as it is woven deeply within our heart. Then we can find compassion and forgiveness.

Practicing Forgiveness

Silent Meditation

Spend ten to twenty minutes in silence, just being present to God. If you choose, you can use a sacred word as your mantra. Simply repeat your word or focus on your breathing.

"Be still and know that I am God" (Psalm 46:10).

Journal Writing

Remember to honor your feelings by not judging them as you experience the pain in your grief and forgiveness process. What do you remember about a person, group, or organization that has hurt you and that you would like to forgive or at least to have a desire to forgive? Your action now is to remember and to write the memory in your journal and to carry that memory in prayer as you knit into God's Word

Do you remember any blessings in your life somehow connected to your hurt? Your action now is to remember and to write the memory in your journal and to carry that memory in prayer as you knit into God's Word.

Take some quiet time with God. Sit with your spine straight, feet on the floor, breathe in deeply, and exhale any tension. *Go to your center.* Relax, breathe, and remember. Allow your memory time to surface. There is no hurry. When ready, pick up your pen and write about the memory that comes to your mind now.

Scripture

Choose one of the following passages of scripture, or choose one of your own favorite sacred texts for knitting into God's Word—lectio divina.

> "But this is the covenant which I will make with the house of Israel after those days, says the Lord. I will place my law within them, and write it upon their hearts; I will be their God, and they shall be my people. No longer will they have need to teach their friends and kinsmen how to know the Lord. All, from least to greatest, shall know me, says the Lord, for I will forgive their evil doing and remember their sin no more" (Jeremiah 31:33–34).

> "Put on then, as God's chosen ones, holy and beloved, heartfelt compassion, kindness, humility, gentleness, and patience, bearing with one another and forgiving one another, if one has a grievance against another; as the Lord has forgiven you, so must you also do" (Colossians 3:12–13).

Knitting into God's Word—Lectio Divina

Preparation

Gather your yarn, needles, and yourself in preparation for being with God in His Word.

Quiet down, be still, silent.

Lectio—Reading

This is a time apart with God. Read scriptures slowly and reverently. Listen with the ear of your heart for the still small voice of God, speaking to you in a word or phrase. That is God's word for you.

Meditatio—Meditation

Once you have found a word or passage in scriptures, take it in, memorize it, and while knitting, gently repeat it to yourself, pondering it in your heart. This is your "knitting meditation."

Oratio—Prayer

God invites you to share with Him your difficult, pain-filled experiences; the unforgiving parts of yourself; and your joys and blessings and to recite gently over them the healing word or phrase He has given you. In this oratio—prayer, you allow your real self to be touched and changed by the Word of God as you gently move your needles.

Contemplatio—Contemplation

Knitting into God's presence, you simply rest in the presence of the One who has used His Word as a means of inviting you to accept His transforming love and forgiveness. Wordless, you rest quietly in the presence of the One who loves you. You practice silence, letting go of your own words, simply enjoying the experience of being in the presence of God while knitting into His Word.

Journal Writing: After Knitting into God's Word—Lectio

Try writing out the word or phrase that spoke to your heart. What is God saying to you right now in this moment? Is He calling you to an action or state of being? Write prayerfully your response to God.

Knitting Prayer

Anytime you pick up your knitting needles today, knit and pray for God's love, forgiveness, and comfort to fill each of your stitches. Pray that your shawl will be a blessing for the recipient and that you will be blessed as you continue on your grief and forgiveness journey.

CHAPTER 6

Gathering: Your Thoughts, Feelings, and Memories

It is through our lives that others will find their way home.[1]

—Paula Huston

In knitting, as in everything else, you learn as much from your mistakes as you do from your successes.[2]

—Pam Ellen

Gather your thoughts and feelings as you write your memories in your journal. They are like many different colors and textures of yarn that sometimes get knotted together. Write to straighten them out, to loosen their clinging together and their clinging to you. As you write your memories inside your journal, you are letting go, loosening your hold on the pain. You are making more room for God.

Susan Zimmerman, in her book *Writing to Heal the Soul*, describes how writing helped her to heal as she wrote about her profoundly brain-injured daughter. Her pain and loss had been submerged inside her very busy life, and when she decided to slow down and reflect by writing about her traumatic loss, she discovered sadness was at her core. Only by writing about it could she finally appreciate life's complex tapestry and embrace her life and everything in it.[3]

James W. Pennebaker, PhD, in his book *Opening Up*, describes the healing power of expressing emotions. He said, "Whether we talk into a tape recorder or write on a magic pad, translating our thoughts into language is psychologically and physically beneficial. Once people can distill complex experiences into more understandable packages, they can begin to move beyond trauma."[4]

Writing in your journal is a helpful, healing tool, a way to remember and to process your feelings. Journal writing brings you in touch with your emotions and even with your physical memories. Then, with more clarity, you can bring them to God in prayer as you knit. Writing your memories can bring you healing and help you to go through the grief and forgiveness process. Through writing, you honor your losses, and you can express your greatest pain and greatest joy. Somehow, through the mystery of God's healing, you can find a light on a path that was dark and little by little, find your way and gain a new perspective. By choosing to remember, you open the door to your deepest truth and allow light to come inside. I believe that in all of your journal stories, especially ones about your grief and loss, God is holding you within His loving embrace.

Practicing Forgiveness

Silent Meditation

Spend ten to twenty minutes in silence, just being present to God, and if you choose, you can use a sacred word as your mantra. Simply repeat your word or focus on your breathing.

"Be still and know that I am God" (Psalm 46:10).

Journal Writing

Remember how you were hurt. Begin anywhere. Start writing without thinking about grammar or making sense. Just keep your pen moving across the page as you remember anything, big or small, that you would like to forgive. Knowing and expressing how you were hurt and what was not okay about what happened to you is important. Forgiveness is for you, not for anyone else. Forgiveness does not mean reconciling with the person or group who hurt you. It is not condoning their action. It is about the peace and understanding that comes from blaming less. You will be surprised at the memories that surface. It is not a test. There are no grades, and no one but you will read your writing. Our memories are selective, and we remember what we need to remember in God's timing. Don't push. Be gentle with yourself, and trust that by desiring to remember, you *will* remember how you actually were hurt.

When you have finished writing about what has hurt you, try to write about a blessing that has touched your life because of or connected to your deep hurt.

Take some quiet time with God. Sit with your spine straight and feet on the floor. Breathe in deeply and exhale any tension. *Go to your center*. Relax, breathe, and remember. Allow your memories time to surface. There is no hurry. When ready, pick up your pen and write about whatever memory or memories come to your mind now.

Scripture

Choose one of the following scripture passages, or choose one of your own favorite texts to use while knitting into God's Word.

> "You have been told, O man, what is good, and what the Lord requires of you: Only to do the right and to love goodness, And to walk humbly with your God" (Micah 6:8).

> "Owe nothing to anyone, except to love one another; for the one who loves another has fulfilled the law. The commandments, 'You shall not commit adultery; you shall not kill; you shall not steal; you shall not covet,' and whatever other commandment

there may be, are summed up in this saying, (namely) 'You shall love your neighbor as yourself.' Love does no evil to the neighbor; hence, love is the fulfillment of the law" (Romans 13:8–10).

Knitting into God's Word—Lectio Divina

Preparation

Gather your yarn, needles, and yourself in preparation for being with God in His Word.

Quiet down, be still, silent.

Lectio—Reading

This is a time apart with God. Read scriptures slowly and reverently. Listen with the ear of your heart for the still small voice of God speaking to you in a word or phrase. That is God's word for you.

Meditatio—Meditation

Once you have found a word or passage in scriptures, take it in, memorize it, and while knitting, gently repeat it to yourself, pondering it in your heart. This is your "knitting meditation."

Oratio—Prayer

God invites you to share with Him your difficult, pain-filled experiences; the unforgiving parts of yourself; and your joys and blessings and to recite gently over them the healing word or phrase He has given you. In this oratio—prayer, you allow your real self to be touched and changed by the Word of God as you gently move your needles.

Contemplatio—Contemplation

Knitting into God's presence, you simply rest in the presence of the One who has used His Word as a means of inviting you to accept His transforming love and forgiveness. Wordless, you rest quietly in the presence of the One who loves you. You practice silence, letting go of your own words, simply enjoying the experience of being in the presence of God, while knitting into His Word.

Journal Writing: After Knitting into God's Word—Lectio

Try writing out the word or phrase that spoke to your heart. What is God saying to you right now in this moment? Is He calling you to an action or state of being? Write prayerfully your response to God.

Knitting Prayer

Any time you pick up your knitting needles today, knit and pray for God's love, forgiveness, and comfort to fill each of your stitches; that your shawl will be a blessing for the recipient and you as you continue on your grief and forgiveness journey.

CHAPTER 7

Holding: God and Your Journal

Compassion is the river that overflows into the ocean of love that has no end; to embrace the suffering of another.[1]

—Ilia Delio, OSF

The act of writing brings a structure and order to the chaos of grief.[2]

—Susan Zimmerman

Holding is a meaningful word in your grief and forgiveness process. It symbolizes your being held by the unconditional love of God, no matter what you have done or had done to you. God holds you and all that you write in your journal, as you once held your babies and or your dearest pets. You know that they are safe and loved, just as you are safe and loved by God. Your journals are an unconditional holding container for all of your emotions and life experiences. They can hold any and all of your human stories, including but not limited to your stories of trauma, loss, forgiveness, or unforgiveness.

Kathleen Adams shares in her book *Journal to the Self* that her journal has been her therapist, available to her twenty-four hours a day. And she can tell this therapist anything. I agree with Kathleen that "we can say all that we want to our journal. We can scream, thrash, wail, rage, celebrate and be funny, accusatory, sarcastic, brilliant, sentimental, cruel, profound, or vulgar. And the cost for this totally accepting and understanding therapist only seventy nine cents!"[3]

What are you holding onto that is taking up too much space in your thoughts? Can you entrust your pain to your journal and clear out some room in your mind and soul for God and His grace? Remember: God is holding you and all that you write!

Practicing Forgiveness

Silent Meditation

Spend ten to twenty minutes in silence, just being present to God and, if you choose, you can use a word from scripture or a word that is spiritually significant as your mantra. Simply repeat your word, or focus on your breathing.

"Be still and know that I am God" (Psalm 46:10).

Journal writing

Write how you were hurt from another perspective—how it could have happened differently. Dr. Fred Luskin teaches in *Forgive for Good* that changing our grievance story just a little can help us heal.[4] Remembering and writing from another perspective means to let go, even just a little bit, to the story you have been replaying in your mind. Remember, your distress comes from the thoughts, hurt feelings, and even physical pain you are feeling right now, not from what offended or hurt you minutes, days, weeks, or years ago.

Take some quiet time with God. Sit with your spine straight and feet on the floor. Breathe in deeply and exhale any tension. *Go to your center.* Relax, breathe, and remember. Allow your memories time to surface. There is no hurry. When ready, pick up your pen and write about whatever memory or memories come to your mind now from a different perspective.

Scripture

Choose one of the following passages from scripture, or choose one
of your own favorite passages to use while knitting into God's Word.

> Not according to our sins does he deal with us,
> Nor does he requite us according to our crimes.
> For as the heavens are high above the earth,
> So surpassing is his kindness toward those who
> fear him.
> As far as the east is from the west,
> So far has he put our transgressions from us.
> As a father has compassion on his children,
> So the Lord has compassion on those who fear him.
> —Psalm 103:10–13

> "Love is patient, love is kind. It is not jealous, (love) is
> not pompous, it is not inflated, it is not rude, it does
> not seek its own interests, it is not quick tempered,
> it does not brood over injury, it does not rejoice over
> wrong doing but rejoices with the truth. It bears all
> things, believes all things, hopes all things, endures
> all things. Love never fails" (1 Corinthians 13:4–8).

Knitting into God's Word—Lectio Divina

Preparation

Gather your yarn, needles, and you in preparation for being with
God in His Word.

Quiet down, be still, silent.

Lectio—Reading

This is a time apart with God. Read scriptures slowly and reverently. Listen with the ear of your heart for the still small voice of God, speaking to you in a word or phrase. That is God's word for you.

Meditatio—Meditation

Once you have found a word or passage in scriptures, take it in, memorize it, and while knitting, gently repeat it to yourself, pondering it in your heart. This is your "knitting meditation."

Oratio—Prayer

God invites you to share with Him your difficult, pain-filled experiences; the unforgiving parts of yourself; and your joys and blessings and to recite gently over them the healing word or phrase He has given you. In this oratio—prayer, you allow your real self to be touched and changed by the Word of God as you gently move your needles.

Contemplatio—Contemplation

Knitting into God's presence, you simply rest in the presence of the One who has used His Word as a means of inviting you to accept His transforming love and forgiveness. Wordless, you rest quietly in the presence of the One who loves you. You practice silence, letting go of your own words, simply enjoying the experience of being in the presence of God, while knitting into His Word.

Journal Writing: After Knitting into God's Word—Lectio

Try writing out the word or phrase that spoke to your heart. What is God saying to you, right now at this moment? Is He calling you to an action or state of being? Write prayerfully your response to God.

Knitting Prayer

Any time that you pick up your knitting needles today, knit and pray for God's love, forgiveness, and comfort to fill each of your stitches, so that your shawl will be a blessing for the recipient and for you, as you continue on your grief and forgiveness journey.

CHAPTER 8

Gleaning: Knitting into God's Word—Lectio Divina

When I found your words, I devoured them; they became my joy and happiness.

—Jeremiah 15:16

I let my knitting become prayer.[1]

—Peggy Rosenthal

The word gleaning reminds me of my childhood visits with my grandparents, aunts, uncles, and cousins on their chicken farm. Glean is a biblical word. It means to gather by the reapers what is left in a garden or field. In biblical times, the corners of one's field were left harvested for the poor and for strangers.[2] I liken gleaning to listening while reading God's Word very slowly while searching for the word or phrase left for us to harvest—lectio divina.

This ancient practice of lectio is one of the precious treasures of Benedictine monastics and oblates. Read until you glean a word or phrase that touches your heart. This is God's word for you today. Meditate on this word, memorizing it and, at the same time, while knitting in prayer, lift up to God your deepest hurt and/or your desire to forgive, as well as any blessings that possibly came to you through your hurt.

Practicing Forgiveness

Silent Meditation

Spend ten to twenty minutes in silence, just being present to God, and if you choose, you can use a sacred word as your mantra. Simply repeat your word or focus on your breathing.

"Be still and know that I am God" (Psalm 46:10).

Journal Writing

Forgiving ourselves is very difficult and painful, especially when we have made a mistake that causes unjust problems for others and ourselves or when we have hurt someone that we deeply care about. It is equally difficult to forgive ourselves when we have not actually done anything but feel responsible for the bad things that have happened to people we care about. We may ask why we weren't there for them. Remember, God loves us and forgives us *no matter what*, and it is through God's grace that we can forgive.

Take some quiet time with God. Sit with your spine straight and feet on the floor. Breathe in deeply and exhale any tension. *Go to your center.* Relax, breathe, and remember. Allow your memories time to surface. There is no hurry. When ready, pick up your pen and write about whatever memory or memories come to your mind now from the perspective of someone you have hurt, and then write about the same memory from your own perspective.

Write now about your choice to forgive or your desire to at least want to forgive. Be mindful that choosing to forgive is a heroic choice.

Scripture

Choose one of the following lines of scripture, or choose one of your own favorite texts to use while knitting into God's Word.

Have mercy on me, O God, in your goodness;
In the greatness of your compassion
Wipe out my offense.
Thoroughly wash me from my guilt
And of my sin cleanse me.

—Psalm 51:3–4

Then the scribes and the Pharisees brought a woman
who had been caught in adultery and made her stand
in the middle. They said to him, "Teacher, this woman
was caught in the very act of committing adultery.
Now in the law, Moses commanded us to stone such
women. So what do you say?" They said this to test
him, so that they could have some charge to bring
against him. Jesus bent down and began to write on
the ground with his finger. But when they continued
asking him, he straightened up and said to them, "Let
the one among you who is without sin be the first to
throw a stone at her." Again he bent down and wrote
on the ground. And in response, they went away one
by one, beginning with the elders. So he was left alone
with the woman before him. Then Jesus straightened
up and said to her, "Woman, where are they? Has no
one condemned you?" She replied, "No one, sir." Then
Jesus said, "Neither do I condemn you. Go, (and) from
now on do not sin any more." (John 8:3–11)

Knitting into God's Word—Lectio Divina

Preparation

Gather your yarn, needles, and you in preparation for being with
God in His Word.

Quiet down, be still, silent.

Lectio—Reading

This is a time apart with God. Read scriptures slowly and reverently. Listen with the ear of your heart for the still small voice of God, speaking to you in a word or phrase. That is God's word for you.

Meditatio—Meditation

Once you have found a word or passage in scriptures, take it in, memorize it, and, while knitting, gently repeat it to yourself, pondering it in your heart. This is your "knitting meditation."

Oratio—Prayer

God invites you to share with Him your difficult, pain-filled experiences; the unforgiving parts of yourself; and your joys and blessings and to recite gently over them the healing word or phrase He has given you. In this oratio—prayer, you allow your real self to be touched and changed by the Word of God as you gently move your needles.

Contemplatio—Contemplation

Knitting into God's presence, you simply rest in the presence of the One who has used His Word as a means of inviting you to accept His transforming love and forgiveness. Wordless, you rest quietly in the presence of the One who loves you. You practice silence, letting go of your own words, simply enjoying the experience of being in the presence of God while knitting into His Word.

Journal Writing: After Knitting into God's Word—Lectio

Try writing out the word or phrase that spoke to your heart. What is God saying to you right now, in this moment? Is He calling you to an action or state of being? Write prayerfully your response to God.

Knitting in Prayer

Any time you pick up your knitting needles today, knit and pray for God's love, forgiveness, and comfort to fill each of your stitches; that your shawl will be a blessing for the recipient and you as you continue on your grief and forgiveness journey.

CHAPTER 9

Transformation

Knitting into the mystery of God.[1]

— Susan S. Izard

A prayer shawl offers a tangible gift of unconditional love.[2]

— Janet Bristow and Victoria A. Cole-Galo

Knitting and praying in God's presence, you can receive God's unconditional love and forgiveness, and then you will become better able to forgive yourself and others. When you knit and pray for or in honor of someone you want to forgive, while saying prayers of forgiveness for that person and/or for yourself, your heart slowly becomes transformed. In the book *Knitting into the Mystery*, Susan Izard describes her experience in the shawl-knitting ministry. "God had engaged us in a great act of compassion. Our knitting was weaving us—our hearts and souls—into the truth of God's love."[3]

Thich Nhat Hanh said in the movie and book *The Power of Forgiveness*, "Forgiveness will not be possible until compassion is born in your heart to forgive."[4] It is in knitting and praying that you can feel compassion and experience God's grace to forgive yourself and those who hurt you. It is the knitting together that our prayers and God's unconditional love bring healing and love to the knitter and to the recipient of our prayers and shawl. In both my Pennsylvania and California prayer shawl ministry groups, we received thank-you cards from many people, who described feeling God's love and comfort when wrapped in their shawls.

Here are a few more stories from my California Prayer Shawl Ministry:

I remember the time when a religious sister at the shelter where we had given shawls had fallen and broken her clavicle, shoulder, and rib. They took her quickly to the hospital and when asked what to bring her, she said, "All I want is my prayer shawl."

A member of our prayer shawl ministry, a religious sister, shared that one day there was a fire in the building where she and many sisters lived, and when they were told to leave the building, she made sure to grab her knitting, not her iPad. They had to relocate, and she was very happy to have her knitting with her.

Another meaningful story for me was the time I knitted an ocean-blue forgiveness prayer shawl for my father on his eighty-third birthday. He said, "This is beautiful. Did you make it for me?" I answered, "Yes, I did, Dad." My father passed away the following year.

I recall also the beautiful smile of a young woman, preparing to be married, and how deeply touched she was when we gave her a prayer shawl.

Another signed her thank-you card: " To the ministry of miracle workers!" Still another recipient said that she was wearing her prayer shawl around the house to ward off the chill, as the nights were getting colder earlier this year.

One dear woman in my church, while undergoing chemo treatments, would take her prayer shawl with her to every treatment.

A thank-you note from the shelter, where we give shawls at Christmas, shared that when the women opened their shawl gifts, they immediately wrapped themselves up in them while they opened the rest of their presents. The shawls were the most meaningful gifts that they received, because the shawls gave the women the assurance and comfort that they were in the right place and doing the right thing with the support of wonderful, prayerful women behind them.

There are so many stories, each one unique, yet each person who received one of our group's shawls described how her prayer shawl brought her comfort. Each one shared how she could feel the prayers and God's love knitted within her shawl when it was wrapped around her shoulders.

Knitting and praying for a person or group you want to forgive or want to have the desire to forgive is what fills a forgiveness prayer shawl. It is one of the most loving gifts you can give to yourself and to another person. God's love is knit into every shawl through your prayers and His Word, and the gift you receive is the softening of your heart as it becomes transformed by God's unconditional love and forgiveness.

Practicing Forgiveness

Silent Meditation

Spend ten to twenty minutes in silence. Just be present to God, and if you choose, you can use a sacred word as your mantra. Simply repeat your word or focus on your breathing.

"Be still and know that I am God" (Psalm 46:10).

Journal Writing

Take some quiet time with God. Sit with your spine straight and feet on the floor. Breathe in deeply and exhale any tension. *Go to your center.* Relax and breathe. There is no hurry. When you are ready, pick up your pen and write about whatever memory or memories come to your mind, about which you feel you need increased compassion and forgiveness. Write now about a memory that called for compassion and/or forgiveness.

Scripture

Choose one of the following passages from scriptures, or choose one of your own favorite texts to use while knitting into God's Word.

> Now that their father was dead, Joseph's brothers became fearful and thought, "Suppose Joseph has been nursing a grudge against us and now plans to pay us back in full for all the wrong we did him!" So they approached Joseph and said: "Before your father died, he gave us these instructions: 'You shall say to Joseph, Jacob begs you to forgive the criminal wrongdoing of your brothers, who treated you so cruelly.' Please, therefore, forgive the crime that we, the servants of your father's God, committed." When they spoke these words to him, Joseph broke into tears. Then his brothers proceeded to fling themselves down before him and said, "Let us be your slaves!" But Joseph replied to them: "Have no fear. Can I take the place of God? Even though you meant harm to me, God meant it for good, to achieve his present end, the survival of many people. Therefore have no fear. I will provide for you and for your children." (Genesis 50:15–21)

> "You have heard that it was said, 'You shall love your neighbor and hate your enemy.' But I say to you, love your enemies, and pray for those who persecute you, that you may be children of your heavenly Father, for he makes his sun rise on the bad and the good, and causes rain to fall on the just and the unjust. For if you love those who love you, what recompense will you have?" (Matthew 6:43–46).

Knitting into God's Word—Lectio Divina

Preparation

Gather your yarn, needles, and you in preparation for being with God in His Word.

Quiet down, be still, silent.

Lectio—Reading

This is a time apart with God. Read scriptures slowly and reverently. Listen with the ear of your heart for the still small voice of God, speaking to you in a word or phrase. That is God's word for you.

Meditatio—Meditation

Once you have found a word or passage in scriptures, take it in, memorize it, and, while knitting, gently repeat it to yourself, pondering it in your heart. This is your "knitting meditation."

Oratio—Prayer

God invites you to share with Him your difficult, pain-filled experiences; the unforgiving parts of yourself; and your joys and blessings and to recite gently over them the healing word or phrase He has given you. In this oratio—prayer, you allow your real self to be touched and changed by the Word of God as you gently move your needles.

Contemplatio—Contemplation

Knitting into God's presence, you simply rest in the presence of the One who has used His Word as a means of inviting you to accept

His transforming love and forgiveness. Wordless, you rest quietly in the presence of the One who loves you. You practice silence, letting go of your own words, simply enjoying the experience of being in the presence of God, while knitting into His Word.

Journal Writing: After Knitting into God's Word—Lectio

Try writing out the word or phrase that spoke to your heart. What is God saying to you right now, in this moment? Is He calling you to an action or state of being? Write prayerfully your response to God.

Knitting in Prayer

Any time you pick up your knitting needles today, knit and pray for God's love, forgiveness, and comfort to fill each of your stitches and that your shawl will be a blessing for the recipient and you as you continue on your grief and forgiveness journey.

A Pattern of Love and Forgiveness: Prayers from the Heart

1. Remembering: the person or group and act that needs to be forgiven
2. Gathering: writing out your memory
3. Holding: God and your journal
4. Gleaning: knitting into God's Word or your favorite text—lectio divina
5. Transformation: knitting, praying, forgiving

Introduction

1. Mirabai Starr, *God of Love* (Rhinebeck, New York: Monkfish Publishing, 2012), 131.
2. Mary Doria Russell, *A Thread of Grace* (New York: Ballantine Books, 2005) 421.
3. Christine Valters Paintner, *Lectio Divina* (Woodstock, Vermont: Skylight Paths Publishing, 2011), x.
4. Christine Valters Paintner, *Lectio Divina* (Woodstock, Vermont: Skylight Paths Publishing, 2011), 4.
5. Christine Valters Paintner, *Lectio Divina* (Woodstock, Vermont: Skylight Paths Publishing, 2011), 5.
6. Fr. Luke Dysinger, OSB, *Accepting the Embrace of God*: Appendix, Knitting Praying Forgiving 62.
7. Susan S. Izard, *Knitting into the Mystery* (Harrisburg, PA: Morehouse Publishing, 2003), 50.
8. Wikipedia contributors, "History of Knitting," *Wikipedia, The Free Encyclopedia*, http://en.wikipedia.org/w/index.php?title=History_of_ knitting&oldid=601951329(accessed June 17, 2014) 1-2.
9. Margaret Guenther, *The Practice of Prayer* (Cambridge Mass.: Cowley Publications, 1998), 26.

Chapter 1—Visits With Anna

1. Lewis B. Smedes, *Forgive & Forget* (New York: Harper Collins Publishers, 1984), 27.
2. John Main, *Knitting into the Mystery* (Harrisburg, PA: Morehouse Publishing, 2003), 14.

Chapter 2—Forgiveness: A Path to Love

1. Mother Teresa, *Knitting for Peace* (New York: Stewart, Tabori & Chang, 2006), 15.
2. Wikipedia contributors, " *Messiah*," *Wikipedia, The Free Encyclopedia*, http://en.wikipedia.org/w/index.php?title=Messiah&oldid=611521311 (accessed June 17, 2014) 1.
3. Mirabai Starr, *God of Love* (Rhinebeck, New York: Monkfish Book Publishing Company, 2012), 64.
4. Elisabeth Kubler-Ross, *On Grief and Grieving* (New York: Scribner, 2005), 7.
5. Dennis Linn & Matthew Linn, *Healing Life's Hurts* (New York: Paulist Press, 1977), 2.
6. Thomas Merton, *The Seven Story Mountain* (New York: Harcourt, Inc., 1948), 186.
7. Catherine de Hueck Doherty, *Poustinia* (Notre Dame, Indiana: Ave Maria Press, 1974), 213.

Chapter 3—Forgiveness Prayer Shawl

1. Jeannette Bakke and Lois Lindbloom, *Praying with a Prayer Shawl* (Northfield, MN: self-published prayer card, 2001).
2. Susan Gordan Lydon, *The Knitting Sutra* (San Francisco: Harper Collins, 1997), 143.
3. Susan S. Izard " Knitting Into The Mystery of God," Presence Journal, September 2000, Vol. 6, No.3.
4. Janet Bristow and Victoria A. Cole-Galo, *Prayer Shawl Companion* (Newtown, CT: Taunton Press, 2008), 5.
5. Susan Gordon Lydon, *The Knitting Sutra* (San Francisco: Harper Collins, 1997), 11.
6. Janet Bristow and Victoria A. Cole-Galo, *Prayer Shawl Companion* (Newton, CT: Taunton Press, 2008), 7.

Chapter 4—Prayers from the Heart

1. Gerald G. Jampolsky, M.D., *Forgiveness The Greatest Healer of All* (Hillsboro, Oregon: Beyond words Publishing,Inc.,1999) xxiii.

2. Bishop Theophany, *Turning the Heart to God* (Ben Lomond, California: Conciliar Press, 2001) 51.
3. John Chryssavgis, *In the Heart of the Desert* (Bloomington, Indiana: World Wisdom, Inc.2003) 45.
4. Loretta Javra, *The Oblate life* (Collegeville, Minnesota: Liturgical Press, 2008) 251.
5. Christine Valters Paintner and Lucy Wynkoop, OSB, *Lectio Divina* (New York/Mahwah NJ: Paulist Press 2008) 2.
6. Susan Gordon Lydon, *The Knitting Sutra* (San Francisco: Harper Collins, 1997), 137.
7. Joan Chittister, *The Rule of Benedict* (New York: Crossroad 2010) 3.

Chapter 5—Remembering

1. Lewis B. Smedes, *Forgive & Forget* (New York: Harper Collins Publishers, 1984), xi.
2. Marvin R. Wilson, *Our Father Abraham: Jewish Roots of the Christian Faith* (Grand Rapids, MI: Wm. B. Erdmans Publishing Company and Dayton, OH: Center for Judaic-Christian Studies, 1989) 153.

Chapter 6—Gathering

1. Paula Huston, *forgiveness following Jesus into radical loving* (Brewster, Massachusets: Paraclete Press 2008) 49.
2. Debbie Macomber, *Knit Together Discover God's Pattern for Your Life* (New York, Boston, Nashville: Faith Words 2007) 45.
3. Susan Zimmerman, *Writing to Heal the Soul* (New York: Three Rivers Press 2002) 15.
4. James W, Pennebaker, PhD, *Opening Up (New York, London: The Guilford Press 1990)* 185.

Chapter 7—Holding

1. Ilia Delio, OSF, *Compassion Living in the Spirit of Saint Francis* (Cincinnati, Ohio: St. Anthony Press 2011) xv.
2. Susan Zimmerman, *Writing to Heal the Soul* (New York: Three Rivers Press 2002) 18.

3. Kathleen Adams, *Journal to the Self* (New York: Warner Books 1990) 5.
4. Fred Luskin, *Forgive for Good* (New York: HarperCollins 2002) 43.

Chapter 8—Gleaning

1. Peggy Rosenthal, *Knit One, Purl a Prayer (Brewster, Massachusets: Paraclete Press 2011)* 13.
2. Wikipedia contributors, "Gleaning, " *Wikipedia, The Free Encyclopedia,* http://en.wikipedia.org/w/index.php?title=Gleaning&oldid=606432800 (accessed June 20, 23014)1.

Chapter 9—Transformation

1. Susan S. Jorgensen and Susan S. Izard, *Knitting into the Mystery of God* (Harrisburg, PA: Morehouse Publishing, 2003), cover.
2. Janet Bristow and Victoria A. Cole-Galo, *Prayer Shawl Companion* (Newtown, CT: Taunton Press, 2008), 143.
3. Susan S. Jorgensen and Susan S. Izard, *Knitting into the Mystery of God* (Harrisburg, PA: Morehouse Publishing, 2003), 15.
4. Thich Nhat Hanh, *The Power of Forgiveness* (Minneapolis, MN: Fortress Press 2008) 25.

Scriptures for Knitting into God's Word: Forgiveness, Love, Compassion

Forgiveness

"You have heard it was said, 'You shall love your neighbor and hate your enemy.' But I say to you, love your enemies, and pray for those who persecute you, that you may be children of your heavenly Father, for he makes his sun rise on the bad and the good, and causes rain to fall on the just and the unjust. For if you love those who love you, what recompense will you have? Do not the tax collectors do the same? And if you greet your brothers only, what is unusual about that? Do not the pagans do the same? So be perfect, just as your heavenly father is perfect." (Matthew 5:43–48)

"When they came to the place called the Skull, they crucified him and the criminals there, one on his right, the other on his left. Then Jesus said, 'Father forgive them, they know not what they do'" (Luke 23:33–34).

"Whoever says he is in the light, yet hates his brother, is still in the darkness. Who loves his brother remains in the light, and there is nothing in him to cause a fall. Whoever hates his brother is in darkness; he walks in darkness and does and does not know where he is going because the darkness has blinded his eyes" (John 2:9–11).

Then Peter approaching asked him, "Lord, if my brother sins against me, how often must I forgive him? As many as seven times?" Jesus answered, "I say to you, not seven times but seventy seven times." That is why the kingdom of heaven may be likened to a king who decided to settle accounts with his servants. When he began the accounting, a debtor was brought before him who owed him a huge debt. Since he had no way of paying it back, his master ordered him to be sold, along with his wife, his children, and all his property, in payment of the debt. At that, the servant fell down, did him homage, and said, "Be patient with me, and I will pay you back in full." Moved with compassion the master of that servant let him go and forgave him the loan. When that servant had left, he found one of his fellow servants who owed him a much smaller amount. He seized him and started to choke him, demanding, "Pay back what you owe." Falling to his knees, his fellow servant begged him, "Be patient with me, and I will pay you back." But he refused. Instead, he had him put in prison until he paid back the debt. Now when his fellow servants saw what had happened, they were deeply disturbed, and went to their master and reported the whole affair. His master summoned him and said to him, "You wicked servant! I forgave you your entire debt because you begged me to. Should you not have had pity on your fellow servant, as I had pity on you? Then in anger his master handed him over to the torturers until he should pay back the whole debt. So will my heavenly

Father do to you, unless each of you forgives his brother from his heart." (Matthew 18:21–35)

He was praying in a certain place, and when he had finished, one of his disciples said to him, "Lord, teach us to pray just as John taught his disciples." He said to them, "When you pray, say: Father, hallowed be your name, your kingdom come. Give us each day our daily bread and forgive us our sins For we ourselves forgive everyone in debt to us, and do not subject us to the final test" (Luke 11:1–4).

We have come to know and to believe in the love God has for us. God is love, and whoever remains in love remains in God and God in him. In this is love brought to perfection among us, that we have confidence on the day of judgment because as he is, so are we in this world. There is no fear in love, but perfect love drives out fear because fear has to do with punishment, and so one who fears is not yet perfect in love. We love because he first loved us. If anyone says, "I love God, but hates his brother, he is a liar; for whoever does not love a brother whom he has seen cannot love God whom he has not seen. This is the commandment we have from him: whoever loves God must also love his brother. (John 4:16–21)

Love

Beloved let us love one another, because love is of God; everyone who loves is begotten by God and knows God. Whoever is without love does not know God, for God is love. In this way the love of God was revealed to us: God sent his only Son into the world so that we might have life through him. In this is love: not that we have loved God, but that he loved us and sent his Son as expiation for our sins. Beloved, if God so loved us, we also must love one another. No one has ever seen God. Yet, if we love one another, God remains in us, and his love is brought to perfection in us. (John 4:7–12)

When he was in Bethany reclining at table in the house of Simon the leper, a woman came with an alabaster jar of perfumed oil, costly genuine spikenard. She broke the alabaster jar and poured it on his head. There were some who were indignant. "Why has there been this waste of perfumed oil? It could have been sold for more than three hundred days' wages and the money given to the poor." They were infuriated with her. Jesus said, "Let her alone. Why do you make trouble for her? She has done a good thing for me. The poor you will always have with you, and whenever you wish you can do good to them, but you will not always have me. She has done what she could. She has anticipated anointing my body for burial. Amen, I say to you, wherever the gospel is proclaimed to the world, what she has done will be told in memory of her." (Mark 14:3–9)

But now, thus says the Lord,
Who created you, O Jacob, and formed you, O Israel:
Fear not, for I have redeemed you;
I have called you by name:
You are mine.
When you pass through water, I
Will be with you;
In the rivers you shall not drown.

When you walk through fire, you shall
Not be burned;
The flames shall not consume you.
For I am the Lord, your God,
The Holy One of Israel, your savior.
I give Egypt as your ransom,
Ethiopia, and Seba in return for you.
Because you are precious in my eyes
and glorious, and because I love you.

—Isaiah 43:1–4

"As the Father loves me, so I also love you. Remain in my love. If you keep my commandments, you will remain in my love, just as I have kept my Father's commandments and remain in his love. 'I have told you this so that my joy might be in you and your joy might be complete. This is my commandment; love one another as I love you. No one has greater love than this, to lay down one's life for one's friends'" (John 15:9–13).

"There was a scholar of the law who stood up to test him and said, 'Teacher, what must I do to inherit eternal life?' Jesus said to him, 'What is written in the law? How do you read it?' He said in reply, 'You shall love the Lord, your God, with all your heart, with all your being, with all your strength, and with all your mind, and your neighbor as yourself.' He replied to him, 'You have answered correctly; do this and you will live'" (Luke 10:25–28).

Compassion

"Put on then, as God's chosen ones, holy and beloved, heartfelt compassion, kindness, humility, gentleness, and patience, bearing with one another and forgiving one another, if one has a grievance against another; as the Lord has forgiven you, so must you also do" (Colossians 3:12–13).

They came to Jericho. And as he was leaving Jericho with his disciples and a sizable crowd, Bartimaeus, a blind man the son of Timaeus, sat by the roadside begging. On hearing that it was Jesus of Nazareth, he began to cry out and say, "Jesus, son of David, have pity on me." And many rebuked him, telling him to be silent. But he kept calling out all the more, "Son of David, have pity on me." Jesus stopped and said, "Call him." So they called the blind man, saying to him, "Take courage; get up, he is calling you. He threw aside his cloak, sprang up and came to Jesus. Jesus said to him in reply, "What do you want me to do for you?" The blind man replied to him, "Master, I want to see." Jesus told him, "Go your way; your faith has saved you." Immediately he received his sight and followed him on the way. (Mark 10:46–52)

I will give thanks to you, O Lord, with all my heart,
(for you have heard the words of my mouth;)
In the presence of the angels I will sing your praise;
I will worship at your holy temple
And give thanks to your name,
Because of your kindness and your truth;
for you have made great above all things
your name and your promise.
When I called, you answered me;
you built up strength within me.
All the kings of the earth shall give thanks to you,
O Lord,

– 74 –

When they hear the words of your mouth;
And they shall sing of the ways of the Lord:
"Great is the glory of the Lord."

—Psalm 138:1–5

Man may be merciful to his fellow man,
But the Lord's mercy reaches all flesh,
Reproving, admonishing, teaching,
As a shepherd guides his flock;
Merciful to those who accept his guidance,
Who are diligent in his precepts.

—Sirach 18:11–13

||||||||||||||||||||||||||||||||||||||||||||||||||||||||||||||||||||||||||||||||||||||||||||||||

Embracing God's Word, Lectio Divina

Accepting the Embrace of God: The Ancient Art of Lectio Divina
by Fr. Luke Dysinger, OSB, SAINT ANDREW'S ABBEY

The Process of Lectio Divina

A very ancient art, practiced at one time by all Christians, is the technique known as *lectio divina*—a slow, contemplative praying of the scriptures which enables the Bible, the Word of God, to become a means of **union** with God. This ancient practice has been kept alive in the Christian monastic tradition, and is one of the precious treasures of Benedictine monastics and oblates. Together with the Liturgy and daily manual labor, time set aside in a special way for *lectio divina* enables us to discover in our daily life an underlying spiritual rhythm. Within this rhythm we discover an increasing ability to offer more of ourselves and our relationships to the Father, and to accept the embrace that God is continuously extending to us in the person of his Son Jesus Christ.

Lectio—reading/listening

The art of *lectio divina* begins with cultivating the ability to **listen deeply**, to hear "with the ear of our hearts," as St. Benedict encourages us in the Prologue to the Rule. When we read the scriptures we should try to imitate the prophet Elijah. We should allow ourselves to become women and men who are able to listen for the still, small voice of God (I Kings 19:12); the "faint murmuring sound" which is God's word for **us**, God's voice touching **our** hearts. This gentle listening is an "atunement" to the presence of God in that special part of God's creation which is the scriptures.

The cry of the prophets to ancient Israel was the joy-filled command to "Listen!" "Sh'ma Israel: Hear, O Israel!" In *lectio divina* we, too, heed that command and turn to the scriptures, knowing that we must "hear"—listen—to the voice of God, which often speaks very softly. In order to hear someone speaking softly we must learn to be silent. We must learn to love silence. If we are constantly speaking or if we are surrounded with noise, we cannot hear gentle sounds. The practice of *lectio divina*, therefore, requires that we first quiet down in order to hear God's word to us. This is the first step of *lectio divina*, appropriately called *lectio*—reading.

The reading or listening which is the first step in *lectio divina* is very different from the speed reading which modern Christians apply to newspapers, books, and even to the Bible. *Lectio* is reverential listening; listening both in a spirit of silence and of awe. We are listening for the still, small voice of God that will speak to us personally—not loudly, but intimately. In *lectio*, we read slowly, attentively, gently listening to hear a word or phrase that is God's word for us this day.

Meditatio—meditation

Once we have found a word or a passage in the scriptures which speaks to us in a personal way, we must take it in and "ruminate" on it. The image of the ruminant animal quietly chewing its cud was used in antiquity as a symbol of the Christian pondering the Word of God. Christians have always seen a scriptural invitation to *lectio divina* in the example of the Virgin Mary "pondering in her heart" what she saw and heard of Christ (Luke 2:19). For us today these images are a reminder that we must take in the word—that is, memorize it—and while gently repeating it to ourselves, allow it to interact with our thoughts, our hopes, our memories, our desires. This is the second step or stage in *lectio divina*— *meditatio*. Through *meditatio* we allow God's Word to become His word for us, a word that touches us and affects us at our deepest levels.

Oratio—prayer

The third step in *lectio divina* is *oratio*—prayer: prayer understood both as dialogue with God; that is, as loving conversation with the One who has invited us into His embrace; and as consecration, prayer as the priestly offering to God of parts of ourselves that we have not previously believed God wants. In this consecration-prayer we allow the word that we have taken in and on which we are pondering to touch and change our deepest selves. Just as a priest consecrates the elements of bread and wine at the Eucharist, God invites us in *lectio divina* to hold up our most difficult and pain-filled experiences to Him, and to gently recite over them the healing word or phrase He has given us in our *lectio* and *meditatio*. In this *oratio*, this consecration-prayer, we allow our real selves to be touched and changed by the word of God.

Contemplatio—contemplation

Finally, we simply rest in the presence of the One who has used His word as a means of inviting us to accept His transforming embrace. No one who has ever been in love needs to be reminded that there are moments in loving relationships when words are unnecessary. It is the same in our relationship with God. Wordless, quiet rest in the presence of the One who loves us has a name in the Christian tradition—*contemplatio*, contemplation. Once again we practice silence, letting go of our own words; this time simply enjoying the experience of being in the presence of God.

The Underlying Rhythm of *Lectio Divina*

If we are to practice *lectio divina* effectively, we must travel back in time to an understanding that today is in danger of being almost completely lost. In the Christian past the words *action* (or *practice*, from the Greek *praktikos*) and *contemplation* did not describe different kinds of Christians engaging (or not engaging) in different forms of prayer and apostolates. Practice and contemplation were understood as the two poles of our underlying, ongoing spiritual rhythm: a gentle oscillation back and forth between spiritual "activity" with regard to God and "receptivity."

Practice—spiritual *activity*—referred in ancient times to our active cooperation with God's grace in rooting out vices and allowing the virtues to flourish. The direction of spiritual activity was not outward in the sense of an apostolate, but **inward**—down into the depths of the soul where the Spirit of God is constantly transforming us, refashioning us in God's image. The *active life* is thus coming to see who we truly are and allowing ourselves to be remade into what God intends us to become.

In contemplation we cease from interior spiritual *doing* and learn simply to *be*, that is to rest in the presence of our loving Father. Just as we constantly move back and forth in our exterior lives between speaking and listening, between questioning and reflecting, so in our spiritual lives we must learn to enjoy the refreshment of simply *being* in God's presence, an experience that naturally alternates (if we let it!) with our spiritual *practice*.

In ancient times contemplation was not regarded as a goal to be achieved through some method of prayer, but was simply accepted with gratitude as God's recurring gift. At intervals the Lord invites us to cease from speaking so that we can simply rest in his embrace. This is the pole of our inner spiritual rhythm called contemplation.

How different this ancient understanding is from our modern approach! Instead of recognizing that we all gently oscillate back and forth between spiritual activity and receptivity, between practice and contemplation, we today tend to set contemplation before ourselves as a goal - something we imagine we can achieve through some spiritual technique. We must be willing to sacrifice our "goal-oriented" approach if we are to practice *lectio divina*, because *lectio divina* has no other goal than spending time with God through the medium of His Word. The amount of time we spend in any aspect of *lectio divina*, whether it be rumination, consecration or contemplation depends on God's Spirit, not on us. *Lectio divina* teaches us to savor and delight in all the different flavors of God's presence, whether they be active or receptive modes of experiencing Him.

In *lectio divina* we offer ourselves to God; and we are people in motion. In ancient times this inner spiritual motion was described as a helix—an ascending spiral. Viewed in only two dimensions it appears as a circular motion back and forth; seen with the added dimension of time it becomes a helix, an ascending spiral by means of which we are drawn ever closer to God. The whole of our spiritual lives were viewed in this way, as a gentle oscillation between spiritual activity and receptivity by means of which God unites us ever closer to Himself. In just the same way the steps or stages of *lectio divina* represent an oscillation back and forth between these spiritual poles. In *lectio divina* we recognize our underlying spiritual rhythm and discover many different ways of experiencing God's presence—many different ways of praying.

The Practice of Lectio Divina

Private lectio divina

Choose a text of the scriptures that you wish to pray. Many Christians use in their daily *lectio divina* one of the readings from the Eucharistic liturgy for the day; others prefer to slowly work through a particular book of the Bible. It makes no difference which text is chosen, as long as one has no set goal of "covering" a certain amount of text: the amount of text "covered" is in God's hands, not yours.

Place yourself in a comfortable position and allow yourself to become silent. Some Christians focus for a few moments on their breathing; other have a beloved "prayer word" or "prayer phrase" they gently recite in order to become interiorly silent. For some the practice known as "centering prayer" makes a good, brief introduction to *lectio divina*. Use whatever method is best for you and allow yourself to enjoy silence for a few moments.

Then turn to the text and read it slowly, gently. Savor each portion of the reading, constantly listening for the "still, small voice" of a word or phrase that somehow says, "I am for you today." Do not expect lightening or ecstasies. In *lectio divina* God is teaching us to listen to Him, to seek Him in silence. He does not reach out and grab us; rather, He softly, gently invites us ever more deeply into His presence.

Next take the word or phrase into yourself. Memorize it and slowly repeat it to yourself, allowing it to interact with your inner world of concerns, memories and ideas. Do not be afraid of "distractions." Memories or thoughts are simply parts of yourself which, when they rise up during *lectio divina*, are asking to be given to God along with the rest of your inner self. Allow this inner pondering, this rumination, to invite you into dialogue with God.

Then, speak to God. Whether you use words or ideas or images or all three is not important. Interact with God as you would with one who you know loves and accepts you. And give to Him what you have discovered in yourself during your experience of *meditatio*. Experience yourself as the priest that you are. Experience God using the word or phrase that He has given you as a means of blessing, of transforming the ideas and memories, which your pondering on His word has awakened. Give to God what you have found within your heart.

Finally, simply rest in God's embrace. And when He invites you to return to your pondering of His word or to your inner dialogue with Him, do so. Learn to use words when words are helpful, and to let go of words when they no longer are necessary. Rejoice in the knowledge that God is with you in both words and silence, in spiritual activity and inner receptivity.

Sometimes in *lectio divina* one will return several times to the printed text, either to savor the literary context of the word or phrase that God has given, or to seek a new word or phrase to ponder. At other times only a single word or phrase will fill the whole time set aside for *lectio divina*. It is not necessary to anxiously assess the quality of one's *lectio divina* as if one were "performing" or seeking some goal: *lectio divina* has no goal other than that of being in the presence of God by praying the scriptures.

Lectio Divina as a group exercise

In the churches of the Third World where books are rare, a form of corporate *lectio divina* is becoming common in which a text from the scriptures is pondered by Christians praying together in a group.[1]

This form of *lectio divina* works best in a group of between four and eight people. A group leader coordinates the process and facilitates sharing. The same text from the scriptures is read out three times, followed each time by a period of silence and an opportunity for each member of the group to share the fruit of her or his *lectio*.

The first reading (the text is actually read twice on this occasion) is for the purpose of hearing a word or passage that touches the heart. When the word or phrase is found, it is silently taken in, and gently recited and pondered during the silence which follows. After the silence each person shares which word or phrase has touched his or her heart.

The second reading (by a member of the opposite sex from the first reader) is for the purpose of "hearing" or "seeing" Christ in the text. Each ponders the word that has touched the heart and asks where the word or phrase touches his or her life that day. In other words, how is Christ the Word touching his own experience, his own life? How are the various members of the group seeing or hearing Christ reach out to them through the text? Then, after the silence, each member of the group shares what he or she has "heard" or "seen."

The third and final reading is for the purpose of experiencing Christ "calling us forth" into *doing* or *being*. Members ask themselves what Christ in the text is calling them to *do* or to *become* today or this week. After the silence, each shares for the last time; and the exercise concludes with each person praying for the person on the right.

Those who regularly practice this method of praying and sharing

---

1   This approach to group *lectio divina* was introduced at St. Andrew's Abbey by Doug and Norvene Vest. It is used as part of the Benedictine Spirituality for Laity workshop conducted at the Abbey each summer.

the scriptures regularly find it to be an excellent way of developing trust within a group; it also is an excellent way of consecrating projects and hopes to Christ before more formal group meetings. A single-sheet summary of this method for group *lectio divina* is appended at the end of this article.

Lectio Divina on life

In the ancient tradition *lectio divina* was understood as being one of the most important ways in which Christians experience God in creation.[2] After all, the scriptures are part of creation! If one is daily growing in the art of finding Christ in the pages of the Bible, one naturally begins to discover Him more clearly in aspects of the other things He has made. This includes, of course, our own personal history.

Our own lives are fit matter for *lectio divina*. Very often our concerns, our relationships, our hopes and aspirations naturally intertwine with our pondering on the scriptures, as has been described above. But sometimes it is fitting to simply sit down and "read" the experiences of the last few days or weeks in our hearts, much as we might slowly read and savor the words of scripture in *lectio divina*. We can attend "with the ear of our hearts" to our own memories, listening for God's gentle presence in the events of our lives. We thus allow ourselves the joy of experiencing Christ reaching out to us through our own memories. Our own personal story becomes "salvation history."

For those who are new to the practice of *lectio divina* a group experience of "*lectio* on life" can provide a helpful introduction. An approach that has been used at workshops at St. Andrew's Abbey is

---

2   Christian life was understood as a gentle oscillation between the poles of *practice* and *contemplation*, as described above; however, contemplation was understood in two ways. First was *theoria physike*, the contemplation of God in creation—God in "the many"; second was *theologia*, the contemplation of God in Himself without images or words—God as "the One." *Lectio divina* was understood as an important part of the contemplation of God in His creation.

detailed at the end of this article. Like the experience of *lectio divina* shared in community, this group experience of *lectio* on life can foster relationships in community and enable personal experiences to be consecrated—offered to Christ—in a concrete way.

However, unlike scriptural *lectio divina* shared in community, this group *lectio* on life contains more silence than sharing. The role of group facilitators or leaders is important, since they will be guiding the group through several periods of silence and reflection without the "interruption" of individual sharing until the end of the exercise. Since the experiences we choose to "read" or "listen to" may be intensely personal, it is important in this group exercise to safeguard privacy by making sharing completely optional.

In brief, one begins with restful silence, then gently reviews the events of a given period of time. One seeks an event, a memory, which touches the heart just as a word or phrase in scriptural *lectio divina* does. One then recalls the setting, the circumstances; one seeks to discover how God seemed to be present or absent from the experience. One then offers the event to God and rests for a time in silence.

Conclusion

Lectio divina is an ancient spiritual art that is being rediscovered in our day. It is a way of allowing the scriptures to become again what God intended that they should be—a means of uniting us to Himself. In *lectio divina* we discover our own underlying spiritual rhythm. We experience God in a gentle oscillation back and forth between spiritual activity and receptivity, in the movement from practice into contemplation and back again into spiritual practice.

Lectio divina teaches us about the God who truly loves us. In *lectio divina* we dare to believe that our loving Father continues to extend His embrace to us today. And His embrace is real. In His word we experience ourselves as personally loved by God; as the recipients of a word which He gives uniquely to each of us whenever we turn to Him in the scriptures.

Finally, *lectio divina* teaches us about ourselves. In *lectio divina* we discover that there is no place in our hearts, no interior corner or closet that cannot be opened and offered to God. God teaches us in *lectio divina* what it means to be members of His royal priesthood—a people called to consecrate all of our memories, our hopes and our dreams to Christ.

APPENDIX: Two Approaches to Group *Lectio Divina*

I) *LECTIO DIVINA* Shared in Community

Listening for the Gentle Touch of Christ the Word
(*The Literal Sense*)
1. One person reads aloud (twice) the passage of scripture, as others are attentive to some segment that is especially meaningful to them.
2. **Silence** for 1–2 minutes. Each hears and silently repeats a word or phrase that attracts.
3. Sharing aloud: [A word or phrase that has attracted each person.] A simple statement of one or a few words. **No elaboration.**

How Christ the Word speaks to *me*
(*The Allegorical Sense*)
4. Second reading of same passage by another person.
5. **Silence** for 2–3 minutes. Reflect on "Where does the content of this reading touch my life today?"
6. Sharing aloud: **Briefly:** "I hear, I see …"

What Christ the Word Invites Me to Do
(*The Moral Sense*)
7. Third reading by still another person.
8. **Silence** for 2–3 minutes. Reflect on "I believe that God wants me to … today/this week."

9. Sharing aloud: at somewhat greater length the results of each one's reflection. [Be especially aware of what is shared by the person to your right.]
10. After full sharing, pray for the person to your right. *Note:* Anyone may "pass" at any time. If instead of sharing with the group you prefer to pray silently, simply state this aloud and conclude your silent prayer with *Amen.*

2) LECTIO ON LIFE: Applying Lectio Divina to my personal salvation history

Purpose: to apply a method of prayerful reflection to a life/work incident (instead of to a scripture passage).

Listening - Gently Remembering
(Lectio—Reading)
1. Each person quiets the body and mind: relax, sit comfortably but alert, close eyes, attune to breathing ...
2. Each person gently reviews events, situations, sights, encounters that have happened since the beginning of the retreat/or during the last month at work.

Gently Ruminating, Reflecting
(Meditatio—Meditation)
3. Each person allows the self to focus on one such offering.
   a) Recollect the setting, sensory details, sequence of events, etc.
   b) Notice where the greatest energy seemed to be evoked. Was there a turning point or shift?
   c) In what ways did God seem to be present? To what extent was I aware then? Now?

Prayerful Consecration, Blessing
(Oratio—Prayer)

4. Use a word or phrase from the scriptures to inwardly consecrate—to offer up to God in prayer—the incident and interior reflections. Allow God to accept and bless them as your gift

Accepting Christ's Embrace; Silent Presence to the Lord
(Contemplatio—Contemplation)

5. Remain in silence for some period.

Sharing our *Lectio* Experience with Each Other
(Operatio—action; works)

6. Leader calls the group back into "community."
7. All share briefly (or remain in continuing silence).

Used by permission of Fr. Luke Dysinger, OSB

Prayer Shawl Card

Created and used by permission of Jeannette Bakke and Lois Lindbloom

PRAYING
WITH A PRAYER SHAWL

*You created my inmost self,
Knit me together in my mother's womb.
For so many marvels I thank you:
a wonder am I,
and all your works are wonders.
Psalm 139:13-14*

PRAYING WITH A PRAYER SHAWL

A prayer shawl is intended to be a reminder of God's ever present love which is as near to you as your own body is to your spirit. It is a gift
for every time and every occasion--joyful or sorrowful,
for every season and circumstance of life--chosen or
unchosen,
when you are weeping or when you are celebrating.

Wear it in times of private prayer. Let it rest on your shoulders as you work or play or read or rest. Wear it to worship. Wear it whenever you are drawn to prayer or when you have no interest in prayer but would like to be reminded of God's loving presence and care.

Invite the Holy Spirit to help you pray. A reading from Scripture may begin your prayer. Let your prayer of worship and your prayers for loved ones, for the world, and for yourself flow naturally in silence or out loud, in writing or singing or drawing.

Wear the shawl however you like. Drape it lightly across your shoulders. Wrap yourself tightly in it or wear it on your head. Cover yourself with it as you rest. Keep it on your favorite chair.

At times you may cling to a prayer shawl because you are clinging to God; you may not want to be far from it. At other times you will touch it only occasionally. You may want to keep it always; or someday you may feel prompted by God to pass it on to someone else.

May you grow in your awareness of God's blessing, resting upon you in all places and at all times, enabling you to be God's person in the world.

A Prayer Shawl Prayer

You created my inmost self,
*   knit me together in my mother's womb.*
For so many marvels I thank you;
*   a wonder am I, and all your works are wonders.*
            Psalm 139 New Jerusalem Bible

In the beginning, Creating God, you formed my being.
You knit me together in my mother's womb.
To my flesh you gave the breath of life.

O Loving One, renew me this day in your love.
Grant me life as a gift of your faithfulness;
Grant me light to journey by;
Grant me hope to sustain me.

May this shawl be for me a sign of your loving, healing
    presence.
May it warm me when I am weary;
May it surround me with encouragement when I am
    discouraged.
May it assure me of your care and comfort when my loved ones
    and I are in pain.
May it remind me that You love me
And that I am surrounded by the prayers of others.

I offer my prayers to you for those I love.
I offer my prayers to you for all who suffer and for the world.

Thank you, God, for this day and for my life.
I offer myself to You for the sake of the world.

Adapted from a prayer by Cathleen Murtha
Presence, Vol. 6: no. 3, September 2000, p. 50

As you receive this prayer shawl, know

that someone prayed while knitting it.

Knitters often report that the rhythmic

motion of the needles helps to quiet their minds and draw

them to prayer and meditation. This prayer

shawl has already helped one person, the person knitter,

to be open to the presence of God.

The knitter also prayed for the one who would

receive the shawl. The knitter-prayer

may not have known who would receive it. Or,

this shawl may have been made especially for you.

The shawl is now yours. May you

experience comfort and peace in the loving

Presence of God.

Text:
Jeannette Bakke, White Bear Lake, MN
Lois Lindbloom, Northfield, MN

Cover Design:
Tonja Clay, Northfield, MN   Fall 2001

GOOD SHEPHERD CATHOLIC CHURCH;
PRAYER SHAWL MINISTRY 2008

Dorothy's Peace and Forgiveness Prayer Card

Dorothy's.. Peace and Forgiveness Prayer Card

Prayer For Peace
Of Saint Francis Of Assisi

Lord, make me an instrument of your peace.
Where there is hatred, let me sow love,
Where there is injury, pardon,
Where there is discord, union,
Where there is doubt, faith,
Where there is error, truth,
Where there is despair, hope,
Where there is sadness, joy,
Where there is darkness, light.
O Divine Master,
Grant that I may not so much seek to be consoled
As to console;
To be understood, as to understand;
To be loved, as to love;
For it is in giving that we receive,
It is in pardoning that we are pardoned,
And it is in dying that we are born to eternal life.

In honor of Dorothy and all people who have lost their life to violence.

For families victimized by acts of violence and murder..

Cheryl is a licensed psychotherapist in private practice for twenty-five years. Her areas of specialty include bereavement, trauma, and personal growth. Cheryl is certified in contemplative spiritual direction. She is a mother, grandmother, and Camaldolese Benedictine Oblate.. Cheryl resides near her family in Los Angeles, California. Visit her at www.knittingprayingforgiving.com

CPSIA information can be obtained at www.ICGtesting.com
Printed in the USA
LVOW11s0016010814

396946LV00001B/2/P